A PAGAN HERO

A PAGAN HERO

AN INTERPRETATION OF MEURSAULT
IN CAMUS' *THE STRANGER*

by Robert J. Champigny

TRANSLATED BY ROWE PORTIS

UNIVERSITY OF PENNSYLVANIA PRESS

PHILADELPHIA

αὔη ψυχὴ σοφωτάτη
καὶ ἀρίστη

HERACLITUS

αἰτίαν δ'ἔχω τῆς τοῦδε
μητρὸς τοῦ φόνου

Apollo, in *The Eumenides*

TRANSLATOR'S NOTE

I wish to express my thanks to Professor Champigny for his invaluable cooperation in preparing this text.

Gratitude is due as well to Donald K. Fry, Jr., Raymond J. Cormier, and Walker Cowen at the University of Virginia; to Norah F. Kasteliz at Editions Gallimard; to Kay Kimble; and especially to Jane Beever, who valiantly unraveled the complications of bringing *Sur un héros païen* into its American edition.

Stony Brook, New York

CONTENTS

A PAGAN HERO

INTRODUCTION

The study which follows takes as its subject the text of *The Stranger*, by Albert Camus, published in 1942. I shall not examine this book as a literary work. I shall place myself within a fiction according to which the reader is in the presence of a narrative made by Meursault, the central character of the book and its narrator in the first person. It is Meursault's character that I propose to study. Understanding of what follows depends upon a previous reading of the novel.

CHAPTER 1

THE STRANGER

The title of the novel is *The Stranger*. One reading allows me to judge that the title was well chosen. Meursault, the narrator, seems to deserve the epithet of "stranger." But in what respect, in what way, is he a stranger?

Imprisoned for murder, Meursault becomes aware, from his lawyer's attitude, that the man does not "understand" him. He then says: "I wanted to assure him that I was like anybody else, absolutely like anybody else." Does Meursault strike me that way, as an ordinary man? Or does he, instead, seem extraordinary? Or both? If he is at once ordinary and extraordinary, is he a stranger to the extent that he is ordinary, or extraordinary? Or is he a stranger through a certain relation of the ordinary to the extraordinary within him?

In relation to what is Meursault a stranger? Is he a stranger wholly, as foreign to reality as he is to society? And in what ways is he a stranger, accidentally or fundamentally? Is he a stranger in his own eyes, in the eyes of other characters, or to the reader of the account? Does Meursault sense his own foreignness, or is it the other characters in the novel who feel he is foreign? Or again, does the reader experience him as a stranger?

My overall impression, that the title of the novel is appropriate, must be made more specific through a re-examination of the text.

A first point can be determined readily: until the time that he is judged in court, Meursault does not in any way regard himself as a stranger. He does not feel foreign in relation to either reality or society.

He does not feel alienated from nature. Instead, he is remarkably suited in temperament to become the accomplice of things. He takes good advantage of the sensual and aesthetic values that his daily encounters and position offer him. In no way does he share the otherworldly Christian sentiment of being cast into a material universe which is in discord with the soul's own nature. The myth of the Fall does not concern him. Nothing could be more remote from Meursault than the lament in the *Salve Regina*: "Exiled, sons of Eve, in this vale of tears."

Nor is Meursault haunted by romantic dissatisfaction. Unlike Christian aspiration, romantic dissatisfaction does not pit the reality of this world against some Divine City. Romantic dissatisfaction does not yearn after something that could be supposed to exist. In pure cases, romantic dissatisfaction is more radical than Christian aspiration: it is dissatisfaction in respect to any world, whether real or possible. Roman-

6

tic dissatisfaction is a thrust toward the impossible. It affectively colors the fact that, by definition, subjectivity cannot wholly be objectified, cannot itself become an object, even a "spiritual" object like the Christian soul. Subjectivity cannot be turned into an objective reality: in order to exist, subjectivity must exist as vocation and desire. Our nature and our dignity consist in this infinite desire. Thus a romantic will feel he is a stranger to the extent that objectivity is fundamentally and intrinsically inadequate to subjectivity.

Meursault shares none of this discontent. He lives happily; the subjective and the objective are in accord. His desires are finite and definite, and in harmony with a finite and definite reality. He is wise, in a common connotation of the word. He may be occasionally "bored," but he is not troubled by romantic ennui. His boredom is finite and determinate, in contrast to an infinite, all-embracing romantic ennui.

Meursault does not feel estranged from society any more than from reality. Here again, he feels at home. Rebellion, disgust, contempt, indignation, and hate do not torment him. His position is well established, a humble one which contents him; thus it is that he rejects an offer to leave his home in Algiers for Paris. He knows, and accepts, the conventions governing his day-by-day relations with other people. Here, for example, is what he says about the manner in which his employer reacted to the news of his mother's death:

"I then thought I shouldn't have said that. Actually, I didn't have to apologize. He should have

7

extended his condolences instead. But he'll probably do that day after tomorrow, when he sees me wearing mourning. Right now, it's almost as if Mother hadn't died. But after the funeral, we'll have shelved this business, and everything will take on a more official look."

The passage is not written ironically. Meursault seems simply to be thinking: "That's the way social matters are." He has some sense of what is or is not suitable to say and do. (When asked whether he wishes to see the body of his mother, he refuses and comments upon his refusal in this way:) "It bothered me because I realized I shouldn't have said that."

If he were totally foreign to the society of men as is, say, a village idiot, he could not put himself in the place of others and imagine their intentions. In particular, he could not interpret words or attitudes as reproachful. But he is sensitive to such things. Speaking about the words addressed to him by the director of the home where his mother had retired, Meursault declares: "I figured he was blaming me for something, so I started to explain things to him." See also what he says about the people who sit up with him at his mother's wake: "For a second I had the ridiculous notion that they were sitting in judgment on me."

He does not feel a stranger in the manner of indifferent men. He enjoys the company of some people. His relationships with women are pleasurable. He has a friendly feeling for his lawyer: "I would have liked to hold him back, and explain that I wanted to have his sympathy. Not so that I would be better

defended but, if I may say so, out of a natural feeling." One of his friends, appearing as a witness for
the defense during the trial, attempts to be as helpful
as possible. Meursault reacts warmly:

"As if he had used up everything he knew and
all the good will he had, Celeste turned to face me.
I thought that his eyes were shining, and that his lips
were trembling. He seemed to be asking me if there
were anything more he could do. I said nothing, and
did not move, but this was the first time I ever felt
the need to kiss a man."

Meursault understands men with temperaments
different from his own. For instance, he understands
the relation between a neighbor and his dog. He also
understands men placed in positions differing from
his, as in the case of his employer:

"Then my boss, naturally, thought I would have
a four-day vacation, counting Sunday, and he couldn't
be very happy about that. But looking at it one way,
it wasn't my fault if they buried mother yesterday
instead of today, and of course I would have had
Saturday and Sunday off anyway. Naturally, that
doesn't keep me from seeing the boss's point of
view."

He also understands—even though it does not
harmonize with his own way of dealing with other
people—the desire of a neighbor to revenge himself
upon a mistress who, he believes, is deceiving him.
"He asked me if I thought she was up to something
(and it was pretty clear to me she was up to something), if I thought she should be punished, and what
I would do in his place. I told him you never know,

but that I did understand why he wanted to make her pay for it."

He takes an interest in what other people say. The banalities recited by the concierge of the old peoples' home do not irritate him: he finds them "true and interesting." He finds a conversation with his closest neighbor similarly interesting. He does not feel estranged in the company of "lowbrows," as would an intellectual.

Yet this is not indicative of an inborn stupidity. He neither feels nor is estranged because of stupidity or ignorance. We learn in passing that he has received some education. He is capable of criticizing a film as "too stupid," and he explains movies to a friend "who doesn't always follow exactly what's happening on the screen." He shows perspicuity in evaluating what he sees. For example, he remarks about people coming out of a theatre that "among them, the boys were moving more excitedly than usual, so I guessed they had just seen an action picture."

He does not feel odd or eccentric. He judges a woman whom he observed in a restaurant as "odd," which shows that he regards himself as a member of the great mass of normal men.

A second point is worthy of notice. Throughout the first portion of the book, characters meeting Meursault do not feel him as a stranger any more than he feels estranged. His employer, of course, finds it odd that Meursault has no ambition, and Marie, the woman with whom he is intimate, finds it odd that he considers marriage as a thing of small importance. Yet these two particular reactions do little to jeopardize Meursault's customary relationships with other men. One declares that Meursault is "a good fellow." Another thinks that Meursault "knows about life," adding that, "men always understand each other." None of the characters coming into contact with him in everyday life makes Meursault feel that he is thought of as a "stranger."

However, from the beginning, Meursault might appear as a stranger to one person: the reader of the novel. The study I have undertaken concerns Meursault and does not consider the book entitled *The Stranger* except as a document, the sole document which I possess about Meursault. In other words, rather than considering Meursault as a character in a novel, I am placing myself inside a fiction according to which the narrative was written by Meursault. In what ways can what Meursault recounts about himself cause him to appear a stranger?

What I have said up to this point is grounded upon a first reading of the book. It has seemed to me that, in the first portion of the book, Meursault does not feel in the least estranged and that other characters do not consider him a stranger. How then, under such circumstances, could he seem a stranger to the reader? Of course I do not wish to assert that Meursault must necessarily seem a stranger: different readers will react differently to him, the same reader can have varied reactions. But I do maintain that Meursault might well appear as a stranger to the reader even though he seems a stranger neither to himself nor to other characters.

This is possible because a special relationship exists between a narrator and a reader. This relationship is not confined to, or at least need not be confined to, a relationship of the everyday type, varieties of which Meursault maintains with human beings during the early part of the book.

What I have examined so far is Meursault's spontaneous life, his day-to-day life as the narrative has led me to envision it. But when I consider the relationship between Meursault and a reader, it is Meursault's elaborated life I am examining, Meursault considered as the narrator of his spontaneous life. From the beginning of the novel, Meursault might very well appear a stranger insofar as he is a narrator. What makes a stranger of him is not so much what he says as what he does not say, or the specific manner in which he expresses what he says and in which he omits what he omits.

In terms of his spontaneous life Meursault comes across to me as an individual perfectly adapted to his natural and social milieu. He takes advantage of what that milieu offers him each day. He is not overwhelmed by his mother's death. Facing that fact, he reacts according to what is commonly termed wisdom: "I thought that just another Sunday was over, that Mother had now been buried, that I was going to get back to work and that, after all, nothing had been changed." His dealings with human beings are easy: no "conflicts" for Meursault, no "complexes," no "problems." Flexibility in adjustment makes him a paradigm of "normality," as popular psychologists employ that term.

But he tells a story. From his spontaneous life, I turn my attention toward his elaborated life, toward a life become language. The reader expects things to be added or subtracted, expects a certain literary decoupage and montage. He expects Meursault to assume the stance of autobiographer. He expects the elimination of trivial details, he expects confidences, certain kinds of analyses, reflections, explanations, interpretations, even judgments. The reader expects to find a bridge permitting him to establish a relationship with Meursault to the extent that he writes about his life. But this bridge is formed only in the final pages of the novel. Meursault plays his role in spontaneous life well, but he might be thought to play his role in the elaborated life ineptly; it may seem that he adapts badly to his role of autobiographer. It is for this reason that, from the beginning of the book, he may seem a stranger in the eyes of the reader.

Meursault appears to be the opposite of Proust. The spontaneous "I" in Proust, the worldly "I," that "I" continually a victim of becoming, may seem a stranger to certain types of readers, to Bergsonian readers for example. But Proust took great pains to establish a complicity between the reader and the "I" of the autobiographer who recalls, reflects, comments, and provides form.

The first part of the narrative ends with an accident in Meursault's life: he kills a man and is imprisoned. It is then that he becomes a stranger to society. He is banished from the human milieu to which he was so well adapted. Having been accepted and provided a kind of protective coloration by private, routine, and profane society, he is banished by official, legal, and religious society. Theoretically, he still has friends, who come to testify for him at the bar: he has not become a stranger to them. But he is a stranger for the judges, for the public, and particularly a stranger for three persons: the interrogating magistrate, the prosecutor, and the prison chaplain.

Meursault is a priori a stranger to the prosecutor, as is any criminal: a prosecutor's mission is to make a scapegoat of any indicted man. The examining magistrate and the chaplain show more discrimination. Both adhere to a Christian conception of life, and with Meursault they are dealing with a purely pagan temperament. In itself, this is not decisive: all they ask of Meursault is to discover standard motives and to make a show of repentance. But not only is Meursault pagan in temperament, he in addition loves veracity. He possesses integrity, he has the dignity of his nature.

Neither of these characteristics, taken separately, is redhibitory. Meursault's pagan temperament allowed him to live in happy and flexible accord with his natural and social milieu. A taste for the exact word and a taste for dignity, on the other hand, do not necessarily exile someone on the condition, as is Meursault's case, that the taste for exactness is limited to an unwillingness to say what is not so. But what makes Meursault seem a stranger to both the examining magistrate and the chaplain is the wedding of both characteristics. It is also this coupling that causes official society to ostracize him, an ostracism which

14

is sanctioned by a condemnation to death. Of course, Meursault killed someone. But there are various kinds of murder. Despite the prosecutor's conventional zeal, Meursault would neither be condemned to die nor be rejected as a monster by theatrical society if he did not unite a temperament which I call "pagan"—according to meanings it will be appropriate to clarify—with a taste for exactness and dignity. For official society tenders extenuating circumstances to the criminal who renders a sincere or an hypocritical homage to conventional values. Meursault's wrongdoing is not so much having committed a crime as it is being, in the eyes of theatrical society, a congenital criminal, a criminal "in the soul." This makes a stranger of him.

A stranger in the eyes of the theatrical society which decides his fate, a scapegoat, a monster, an objective stranger, Meursault is little by little transformed into a stranger in his own eyes; he feels himself a stranger, he subjectively becomes a stranger.

This transformation is slow, gradual. It is only after judgment has been pronounced and when the chaplain comes to annoy him in the cell that Meursault assumes openly and subjectively the condition of stranger that has been created for him. Yet at the same time, Meursault's reaction to the chaplain's intervention can be interpreted as his refusal to become a total stranger, that is, as a refusal to become a stranger to himself and to his own life.

The bargain which the chaplain proposes is the following: Meursault has been rejected by human society, and this rejection will ultimately be expressed by his death. But at least if Meursault repents, it is possible for him not to be cast away by God, not to be a stranger in the eyes of the Christian God.

At first sight, this does not even seem to describe a bargain. If one reasons after the manner of Pascal, what would Meursault be obligated to contribute, what has he to lose? It is, however, a bargain, and Meursault indeed has something to lose: his pagan dignity is in jeopardy. (A Christian would say his "pride." Whoever does not bow low before the Christian God displays Satanic pride.)

Meursault reacts angrily. He realizes that the chaplain is asking him to repudiate his philosophy of life, his morality, his integrity. In order to avoid being cast out as a stranger by a certain god, Meursault would be forced to make a stranger of himself, a stranger to his life as he has lived it:

"He seemed so very certain, didn't he? Yet none of his certitudes was worth one hair on a woman's head. He was not even certain about being alive because he was living like a dead man. As for myself, I seemed empty-handed. But I was certain about myself, certain of everything, surer than he, certain about my own life and about that death that was going to come. I had nothing except that, but at least I was holding this truth as much as it was holding me."

Thus Meursault refuses to repudiate his own life. So doing, he deliberately and definitively cuts himself away from theatrical and religious society, from the society which represents *antiphysis*. At the same time, suddenly taking hold of his almost completed life, or at least of the idea of a life almost completed, as though he held it in his hands, he communes with himself, and with his life as it participates in *physis:*

"And so did I feel ready to relive everything. It seemed this great anger had purged me of evil and emptied me of hope and, facing the night filled with signs and stars, for the first time I opened myself up to the tender indifference of the world."

I have attempted to show briefly how Meursault was and was not a stranger. The results may be enumerated in the following manner:

Meursault refuses theatricality, *antiphysis.* He attempts to become one with spontaneity, with *physis.* Meursault rejects the hope of entering a Divine City, a city conceived as the pre-eminent *antiphysis.* He has been rejected by theatrical society, that is by society not as it is made up of natural beings but by society in its consecrated hypocrisy. And does not his ineptitude at assuming the role of autobiographer also define him as a stranger to theatricality?

What becomes of the relationship between the reader and Meursault during the second part of the novel? I posited a reader in whose eyes the narrator Meursault would appear a stranger. When the second part begins, when Meursault is interrogated by the examining magistrate, the reader becomes aware that the narrative he has read is equivalent to the declarations of Meursault facing his judges. And the reason Meursault has appeared a stranger in the reader's eyes is more or less the same reason that he is going to seem a stranger in the eyes of his judges. In his

17

role of the indicted man, Meursault will reveal the same rejection of theatricality as in his role as autobiographer; and so, the reader who saw Meursault as a stranger now feels that he has become an accomplice of Meursault's judges.

This fact probably would not disturb a certain kind of reader who would not mind this complicity and fall into step with the examining magistrate, the prosecutor, and the chaplain. There might even exist a reader who, as Meursault wishes, would greet him on the day of his execution "with cries of hate." It is best to maintain silence regarding this type of reader. Let us instead envision the case of a reader less restricted in viewpoint and less hypocritical.

For the reader who initially sensed a stranger in Meursault, the second portion of the narrative can bring about an alteration in judgment. As Meursault is rejected by religious and theatrical society, as he objectively becomes a stranger and, in consequence, subjectively feels a stranger, this reader can sense an attraction toward Meursault, can feel with him.

"With him" may simply imply an undiscriminating sympathy. When an individual and society conflict, sympathy is directed with ease toward the individual because the individual is weaker. We experience compassion for someone who is suffering, for someone who, like Meursault, is going to die.

But the phrase "because the individual is weaker" is not overly satisfying and, with some reflection on the subject, one might find an attitude of sympathy more enlightened than simple compassion. After all, there are occasions where it is the stronger who attracts sympathy (though not pity). In order to find a valid reason for sympathy, one must discard both weakness and strength.

Sympathy is properly directed toward an individual, weak or strong, to the extent that the individual embodies individuality, or better uniqueness, in other words, the very foundation of value. Because I have a single life to live, a life that no one else can live in my stead, various phenomena will be stamped with value for me. Hence my sympathy will go properly toward someone who embodies uniqueness, to someone who provides an echo of my own singularity. If what embodies uniqueness to me is struck down, there will be pity or anger; if what embodies uniqueness is triumphant, there will be admiration and joy.

My conception of life may be greatly different from Meursault's (as in fact it is). That does not make it less true that for me—and I would suppose that the case is similar for other readers—Meursault embodies uniqueness, authenticity, value, as opposed to the prosecutor and chaplain who embody social and religious convention, inauthenticity, nonvalue.

And the sympathy that I bear Meursault, a sympathy which tends toward a certain kind of identification, is not mere sympathy for a victim, is perhaps not that at all. On the last pages of the novel, my sympathy becomes admiration for the hero, for Meursault then is a hero. A hero, Meursault becomes a stranger in solitude, he is alone within his narrative; he has even become a stranger to that narrative. But it is then also that the reader can best rejoin Meur-

19

sault; it is here also that those traits about Meursault which most readily rendered him a stranger in the eyes of the reader have most opportunity of being erased.

Briefly in this chapter I have presented the themes that I am about to develop in the following manner:

First I shall analyze Meursault's salient traits; I shall see in him an innocent man and a just one. Then I shall show how these characteristics contribute to making a guilty man of him in the eyes of theatrical and religious society. Finally I shall examine how, because of his reaction to his predicament, Meursault may be termed a hero.

CHAPTER 2

INNOCENCE

The reader of Meursault's narrative often has the impression of dealing with a candid and thoughtful child. Meursault has maintained the virtues of childhood, spontaneity in particular. He has not fallen into adulthood. He possesses the virtues of childhood and not its vices, for instance the vice of mimicry which makes a preadult out of a child. He has maintained the virtues of childhood, not the virtues of adolescence: Meursault is no romantic.

Meursault's horizon is childlike. Space for him is limited to what he encounters each day. Time is limited to the moment, to a day, to the next day, to a week at most. He does not turn his thoughts toward the past: it is only during his period of testing in prison that he attempts to make use of memories. He appears as an individual without a past, as a flat and transparent strip of glass.

When the prosecutor exploits the fact that Meursault has never "expressed any regrets," Meursault remarks: "I would have liked to try explaining to him cordially, almost affectionately, that I never really had been able to regret anything. I was always absorbed by what was going to happen that day or the day after it."

He easily abstracts himself from an unpleasant day in order to dream about more agreeable things awaiting him. Returning from his mother's funeral, he tells of his "joy when the bus entered the nest of lights of Algiers, and when I thought that I was going to go to bed and sleep for twelve hours."

His need of sleep and his aptitude for falling asleep when a waking moment offers him nothing of interest, this animal wisdom, may similarly be indicative of childish traits. We see him sleep in the bus which is taking him to the asylum where his mother has died, we see him sleep during the wake for his mother, and he falls asleep on the beach. In prison he manages to sleep "about seventeen or eighteen hours a day."

The desire to enjoy the moment goes with his horror of wasted time. The comedy of his trial, this adult comedy to which he is subjected, enters into his category of wasted time. He prefers sleeping to participating as his role of the indicted criminal demands: "All the useless things I was doing in this place rose to my throat again, and all I wanted was for it to be over so I could get back to my cell and sleep."

If a moment is wasted and if he cannot sleep, he has nothing left but boredom. It is not a question, as I have already noted, of romantic ennui, but of a childlike boredom, in terms of a particular moment:

"He was boring me a little, but I had nothing to do and I was not sleepy."

Instead of collecting stamps he clips certain things from the newspapers: "Somewhat later, in order to have something to do, I took an old newspaper, and read it. I cut out an advertisement for Kruschen salts and pasted that into an old notebook where I put things from the papers that amuse me." This happens on a Sunday, a day which Meursault dislikes, as French children generally do.

I have already mentioned his acceptance, and in certain cases his understanding of, social conventions and proprieties. Here again he adopts a childlike attitude. A child adopts and sometimes understands the rules and conventions of adult society. But (at least if we are discussing a healthy child) he does not internalize these rules; he assumes no responsibility for them. Meursault's use of the expression "not my fault" is revealing. He is aware of the responsibility with which he is charged, but aware of it as something conventional and objective. He knows, rather than assumes, this responsibility. He knows that he is held to be a responsible person; but he does not feel responsible himself in cases which concern the observance of convention:

"I told her that Mother had died. As she wanted to know how long ago, I answered, 'It was yesterday.' She seemed embarrassed, but said nothing. I wanted to tell her that it was not my fault, but I caught myself because I remembered I had already said that to my boss. It could mean nothing. In any case, one is always somewhat at fault."

Like a child he experiences difficulty in managing conventional formulas. When characterizing the attitudes of other people toward him he uses two adjectives, of which the second especially strikes a childish note: "nice" and "mean." He finds a man with whom he is walking "very nice" to him. During his contentions with "justice" he appreciates moments when people "are not mean" to him. The attitude and the words of the prosecutor cause him to say, "I had a stupid need of crying because I felt how much those men detested me."

But people can also approach him as companions in a game, as individuals with whom it is possible to maintain natural, authentic relationships. Swimming in the sea with Marie, he experiences that concord only a well-played and wordless game may establish: "The water was cold and I was happy to be swimming. Marie and I swam away together from the beach and I felt that we greatly shared our moving together, and were content."

Yet Meursault is not a child, or rather, from the point of view I have chosen, he is not just a child. Maintaining the virtues of childhood while eliminating its vices implies reflection and a kind of training. The narrative contains one allusion concerning this point. This allusion permits the inference that Meursault was tempted during his adolescence, that he came close to falling into adulthood. His employer has just reproached him for having no ambition. Meursault then makes what is almost his only confidence about his past: "When I was a student I had

24

a good deal of that kind of ambition. But when I had to give up studying, I very quickly realized that all that had no real importance."

Thus Meursault has shaped a certain conception of life, one differing from that of almost all other adults, who are content with the conception which was prompted into them. Meursault's conception will be explicitly and openly assumed on the last page of the narrative.

I have already spoken of Meursault's "pagan" temperament. It is appropriate to clarify what I mean by that term. Meursault's paganism will be presented as a development of what I have called the virtues of childhood. The Greeks have often been compared to children. What I have said so far about Meursault may recall the words of Nietzsche, according to whom the Greeks were superficial because they were deep. But these remarks are not adequate to clarify the meaning I propose to give to the word "pagan."

I indicated previously that by "pagan" I mean non-romantic and non-Christian. I have remarked that romantic dissatisfaction, the sense for and desire after the infinite, an infinite desire, a sentiment of the disproportion between the subjective and the objective, the sense that subjectivity is the fundamental mystery, that all this which is eminently romantic is not in the least applicable to Meursault.

Unbounded desire cannot generally be content with the offerings of perception. A romantic turns back to memory, toward poetic memory, to nostalgia: the word *Sehnsucht* means both nostalgia and desire. Now, I have remarked that Meursault is not pre-

25

occupied with memories except during his hours of imprisonment, and that he is preoccupied then, not by nostalgia, but by particular memories, by memories which he might turn to practical use. Romanticism also makes a cult of the imagination: the word "imagination" is doubtlessly the best rallying-banner for romantics. Meursault admits, on the other hand, "I never had a real imagination." The images that he attempts to call forth in his cell are precise, and he has a practical purpose in mind. Meursault is a "realist." He is interested primarily in what is perceived, in whatever presents itself concretely to him at a given moment. If what presents itself is poor or disagreeable, "boring," he calls upon sleep. If he cannot sleep, then only and as a last expedient does he resort to memory or fancy. Poetic, creative exaltation, which is at the heart of romanticism, is foreign to him.

The distinction between "pagan" and "romantic" counts little for the rest of this study. On the other hand, I must at greater length make the distinction between "pagan" and "Christian" explicit. My intention is to present in terms of that perspective the opposition between Meursault and formal society, in particular the opposition between Meursault and the examining magistrate, then the chaplain.

In describing the conception that Meursault develops of life as "pagan," I refer to Greek thought. But so general a reference is inadequate because Greek thought is very diverse. It was by building upon certain Greek thinkers that Christianity grew into a theology. Moreover, if one abandons philosophy for mythology, one finds in Greek literature myths which do not lack resemblance to the Judeo-Christian myths of Creation, the Fall, of afterlife and judgment. Finally, the word "Christian," after so many centuries of evolution, ramification, and compromise, has become able to signify almost anything, and no matter what. To present an example of some import to this study, should I consider the words attributed to Jesus, "Who is my mother?" as marked with the Christian spirit; or am I instead to credit the authority of the cult of the family, particularly the person of the mother, which the Christian priests have encouraged? Another example: Jesus is said to have counseled his disciples to become as children. But I have suggested that by maintaining the virtues of childhood Meursault had implicitly taken up with a pagan conception of life.

My intention in using the words "pagan" and "Christian" is not to define paganism as one category and Christianity as an opposite category, a task before which the historian of ideas would recoil. To justify my use of the two terms, suffice it that I shall present on one side a grouping of ideas which can be recognized as clearly pagan and not Christian, and on the other a second grouping which can be recognized as clearly Christian and not pagan. I do not presume to reach the essence of either paganism or Christianity, assuming that they can have an essence. In order to avoid misunderstanding, I shall speak in terms of "my pagan" and of "my Christian."

The notion basic to "my" pagan is that of *physis*. He both affirms *physis* and questions it. Physis is all-embracing, opposed by nothing, at least on the fundamental plane. My pagan participates in the order of this physis, yet he can emerge from it, separate himself from it, and manifest it badly, thus placing himself in a state of "unrighteousness." My pagan's moral principle is the following: live according to physis.

My Christian minimizes the import of the notion of physis, or rather he retains no sense of it. Physis for him becomes nature, and that nature is interpreted as the creation of a being called God. My Christian partakes both of nature and of the divinity. He was created in the same way as other creatures, but God created him in His image. What once was physis for my pagan is divided into spirit and matter, or into soul and flesh. My Christian's existence in the midst of matter is the consequence of the "Fall" of his earliest ancestor. My Christian feels that he is an exile within material nature. This split between my Christian and nature is borne out by the myth of Incarnation and redemption. God made Himself into human flesh in order to save my Christian, though not the animals or the plants. The paradise to which my Christian aspires is an *antiphysis,* a Society, a Divine City.

My Christian's God is personal. He is not simply the divine. The domain of persons takes form apart from the rest of creation. A moral order is distinguished from the natural order. There are natural laws, and then there are ethical commandments.

In order to distinguish what is a person from what is not a person, my Christian speaks of the soul. My Christian's soul is quite different from the psyche of my pagan. My Christian has not arrived at a pure conception of subjectivity: he is not a Romantic. If the soul of my Christian is not an object for other persons, at least it is a "spiritual" object, an object of knowledge for his God. My Christian's soul is midway between my pagan's psyche and a romantic subjectivity.

My pagan defines himself as an animal endowed with logos: my Christian is defined as a fallen soul. From the beginning, my pagan feels innocent; from the beginning, my Christian feels guilty. My Christian is responsible for his soul in the eyes of his God. My pagan is responsible in his own eyes insofar as he possesses logos, that is, intellect and language. By the use of this logos, he may grow in tune with physis, or grow out of accord with it. So far as he is in accord, my pagan is a sage. My Christian attempts to resemble his God. If he succeeds, he is a saint.

My pagan is in pursuit of happiness, the means for which is a knowledge of physis. The love of wisdom is a love of knowing or of comprehending, and its end is happiness. A moral fault is not distinguishable from an intellectual fault. It is caused by error and ignorance. Unhappiness is the result of a discord; it is not always traceable to bad luck.

The morality of my Christian is not one of happiness. His morality is ambiguous. It can be interpreted as a morality of duty: my Christian's duty is to attempt to resemble his God, and his method is to obey the commandments attributed to his God. My Christian's morality may also be interpreted as an ethics of salvation: his goal is beatitude after death. The redemption of my Christian is not dependent upon his obeying the ethical commandments that he attributes to his God. His salvation depends upon faith in Jesus Christ, because through the power of Christ my Christian can be saved. It is not so much in terms of virtue as in terms of how a sinner believes and repents that my Christian may gain his salvation: the God of my Christian loves repentance. Thus what is efficacious is not knowledge or comprehension, but belief and repentance. However, my Christian can never be certain of his salvation, for it is supposed that God alone is able to judge his soul. The God who judges is a personal God, capable of intervention into the natural order which He created: providence, grace, ordeal.

Meursault is in clear opposition to two characters who profess Christianity, the examining magistrate and the chaplain. Among pagan doctrines, that of Epicurus is probably the one which Christians found most unfavorable. Meursault's temperament is Epicurean, though of course not in the vulgar meaning of the term. And his morality is Epicurean.

In composing "my pagan" I have relied upon Epicureanism. But, while it allows me to characterize Meursault's temperament and his wisdom, the Epicurean schema is not wholly adequate. For me, the atmosphere of the narrative occasionally evokes tragic and Ionian echoes.

Having laid the foundations of the "pagan" schema, I am now in a position to describe Meursault's character, his temperament, his morality, and his conception of life in a coherent manner.

Negatively, Epicurean happiness consists of the absence of physical and mental suffering: aponia and ataraxia. Positively, happiness consists of pleasure, in "the judgment of nature itself, when nothing has already depraved it, and when it is expressed in all its purity and naïveté." It is a question of maintaining one's innocence and spontaneity.

Epicurus distinguishes between natural and necessary desires, natural but unnecessary desires, and unnatural and unnecessary desires. These last are practiced in the field of social antiphysis, of formal society: ambition, vanity. It is fitting to divest oneself of these parasitical desires in order to pursue the satisfaction of natural desires. In an ordinary situation, this is not difficult: "Nature is easily contented by limited goods, which are few in number and easy to acquire."

Meursault has divested himself of unnatural desires. This is shown in a passage already cited: "When I was a student, I had a good deal of that kind of ambition. But when I had to give up studying, I realized very quickly that all that had no real importance."

Expressions such as "I don't care" or "of no importance" occasionally encountered in the narrative might give the impression that Meursault is totally indifferent. In fact, one ought to speak of ataraxia rather than indifference, one ought to speak of an absence of perturbation. Meursault can seem indifferent only because he has become disentangled from unnatural desires, and it is these unnatural desires which ordinarily are described in written language. These desires, being social, are closely tied in with

31

the emergence of the language of communication (though not of the language of pure and simple expression).

Meursault is not encumbered with ambition. Similarly, he seems devoid of vanity, though not of dignity: he has no social vanity, and his dignity is natural. He could not be troubled with that unnatural desire to marry which preoccupies Marie, nor could he, like Marie, consider marriage as a grave thing.

Meursault has razed useless superstructures within himself. Passion (excepting a fundamental passion which reveals itself to him after his condemnation to death) does not threaten to compromise his ataraxia, his openness to concrete reality. Marie asks him if he loves her. He answers negatively because he understands that by "love" Marie means something other than liking. Meursault is not in the least indifferent, even where people are concerned. For example, he tells his lawyer that he was fond of his mother and that he wishes that she had not died. But his mother's death did not overwhelm him: "I explained to him that my nature was such that my physical needs often got in the way of my feelings. The day we buried Mother I was worn out and very sleepy."

A better expression of this is that sentiments do not interfere with his physical demands, that passions do not trouble his ataraxia, that social desires are not substituted for his natural desires. What are Meursault's natural desires? Hunger, thirst, sleep. Natural still, though unnecessary (as he discovers in prison), is a desire to smoke, and the desire for physical love.

Basically there is a desire not to suffer physically, the desire for aponia.

In the course of his narrative Meursault conscientiously notes his pleasures and his vexations: his liking for *café au lait* and the quality of the coffee offered him by the concierge at the rest home, the cigarettes he smokes, his stiffness and fatigue during the wake, an aching back here and an aching neck there, the pleasures of rest, of swimming, and of lunching on the beach. The following is reminiscent of Socrates deriving pleasure from scratching:

"Before leaving the office for lunch, I washed my hands. At noon I like this moment. Evenings, I enjoy it less because the rolling towel that the machine uses is quite damp from being used all day. One day I brought this to the boss's attention, and he answered that he was sorry but that it was, after all, a rather unimportant detail."

What is important to the employer is ambition, and not the quality of the towel. The social theatre is important to the employer, though concrete reality is not.

Meursault does not consider himself an actor among other actors on the social scene so much as a living individual among living individuals in the midst of nature. He places a neighbor and his dog on the same plane as living creatures: "They seem to belong to the same race, and yet they hate each other. . . . For eight years they have not changed the course of their daily walk. . . . They both stop on the sidewalk and watch each other, the dog with terror, the man with hate."

Meursault is sensitive not merely to what is usefully pleasant, he is also sensitive to aesthetically pleasant things. He is sensitive not only to a particular phenomenon, he is sensitive to atmosphere, to the present totality out of which a particular thing emerges. His glance is inclusive as well as divisive. Meursault is penetrated by physis in its encompassing presence. At such times he is reminiscent of the Ionian vision. This sensitivity to a fundamental physis in its totality and in its power makes it possible for Meursault's life to be something other than a scattered collection of pleasures and boredoms, of isolated facts. This sensitivity will permit his life to take form within a tragic destiny, and will also permit Meursault to assume this unification of his life, that is, to become a hero.

During a court session, Meursault is withdrawn from the unreality about him by memories "of a life that belonged to me no longer, but in which I had found the simplest and most persistent of my joys: odors of summer, the neighborhood I liked, a certain evening sky, Marie's laugh and her dresses."

Let us single out the sky from this catalogue of pleasures. The reference is made over and again in Meursault's narrative. We are constantly aware that facts and things are placed in the framework not of the theatre, but of nature. Meursault spends the afternoon and evening of one Sunday contemplatively at his window, looking over human appearances in the street, appearances and disappearances coinciding with the passage of the day.

As in the Ionian view, the major presences in the

narrative of this townsman are the sky and the sea, night and day, and above all sun and sunlight: "I was blinded by a sudden splashing of light. . . . The brimming sunlight that made the countryside quiver rendered it inhuman and depressing. . . . I remained for a long time watching the sky. . . . I had the whole of the sky in my eyes and it was blue and gold. . . . The sky was green, and I felt happy. . . . It was good to feel the summer night flowing on our brown bodies. . . . Day, already full of sunlight, struck me like a slap. . . . The sunlight was falling almost from directly above on the sand, and its brilliance on the sea was unbearable. . . . The sunlight now was crushing. . . . I stayed at the first step, my head ringing from the sunlight, discouraged in advance by the effort it would require to climb the wooden stairway and to approach the women. But because of the heat it was as painful to remain unmoving under the blinding rain of heat which fell from the sky. . . . I strained to overcome the sunlight and the opaque drunkenness that it poured over me. . . . An entire beach vibrant with sunlight crowded behind me. . . . A burning sword gnawed at my eyelashes and dug into my stinging eyes. Then everything lurched. The sea poured forth a thick and ardent breath. It seemed to me that the sky was opening over its entire expanse to let loose a sheet of flame. . . . The harsh light which poured into the windows from the sky and glanced around in the room. . . . Facing that night filled with signs and stars, I was opening myself up for the first time to the tender indifference of the world."

It can be seen that Meursault is not always capable of enduring the violence of physis, of maintaining his place within it. There will be error and tragedy. Meursault's tragedy, from the crime through its "analysis," its liberating assumption, is social only in appearance. Meursault must reject this appearance in order to assume the natural tragedy which is authentically his own.

Meursault adjusts to his imprisonment according to a wisdom which again might be called Epicurean:

"I would wait for the daily walk that I made in the courtyard, or my lawyer's visit. The rest of my time was very well managed. I often thought then that if I had been forced to live in the dry trunk of a tree, with nothing to do except watch the bloom of the sky above my head, I would little by little have grown accustomed to it. I would have waited for the flocking of birds and the blending of clouds as now I would await those strange neckties my lawyer wore and as, in another world, I used to endure things until Saturday when I could clasp Marie's body. Now, to be fair about it, I was not passing time in a dried-up tree. There were people worse off than myself. That was one of Mother's ideas, and she had repeated it very often, that one gets used to anything in the end."

In his cell, he fights boredom by making an imaginary tour of the room in which he had lived:

"I tried not to lose the thread of my inventory, to make a complete count. So that at the end of several weeks, I could spend hours just enumerating what was in my room. Thus, the more I reflected, the more forgotten and unappreciated things I could bring forth out of my memory. Then I understood that a man who has lived no longer than a single day could easily live a century in prison. He would build up enough memories to avoid boredom."

But Meursault encounters a fundamental difficulty when the death sentence has been passed against him. He still attempts to reason with himself, to continue the tactic which has succeeded up till now. He thinks of his petition for mercy:

"I always took the darkest possibility: my appeal had been turned down. 'All right, so I die.' Earlier than other people, that was evident. But everybody knows that life is not worth living. And I knew that whether you die at thirty or at sixty matters very little. . . . At that moment, what bothered me somewhat in my line of reasoning was the frightening leap I felt in myself at the thought of having twenty more years to live. But I could stifle that by thinking what my thoughts would be twenty years from now when I arrived at this same point. Since everyone dies, the how and the when do not matter, that is obvious. Thus (and the difficult thing was not losing sight of all the reasoning that this 'thus' represented), thus I had to accept the rejection of my appeal.

"At that moment, at that moment only, I had, so to speak, the right, I gave myself permission to approach a second hypothesis: I was pardoned. The vexing thing about that was that I had to make the bound of my body and my blood—that spring which made my eyes smart with a mad joy—less ardent. I had to apply myself to lessening this cry, to reasoning. I had to be natural even in this second hypothesis, in order to make my resignation about the first more plausible. When I had succeeded, I would have gained an hour of calm. This was not to be ignored."

Meursault's wisdom here combats a difficulty of a special order. He has divested himself of particular passions. No passion for a defined object has gravely menaced his ataraxia. But now Meursault discovers in himself a passion for the total object, for the total object which is also a subject, which is himself as a living being: the passion to live. If, in the concluding pages of the novel, he manages to overcome this major obstacle, it is not in the manner that his Epicurean wisdom has triumphed over other ordeals. Epicurus emphasized the problem of the fear of death, but he may not have treated it in a fitting perspective.

Meursault will not strip himself of this passion to live, for it is the basis of his integrity. To adopt a purely Epicurean wisdom here would probably be to deny himself. Meursault maintains the exaltation of living: he will try to make himself equal to it. It seems to me that at such a time Meursault transcends the limits of wisdom: he becomes a hero. We are not yet in a position to approach that final Meursault.

In this chapter I was interested, above all, in analyzing and characterizing Meursault's temperament, what he was spontaneously rather than what he wanted to be. But I have been led, especially nearing the end of the chapter, to touch upon his conception of life. Confining oneself to the study of what is spontaneous and implicit quickly becomes artificial unless one also appeals to what is thought, voluntary, and explicit, all the more so because the materials at our disposal are drawn from Meursault's narrative. Let us now examine directly the thinking, willing, explicit Meursault. From the simple living individual let us turn to a living being endowed with logos, from innocence to justness.

CHAPTER 3

JUSTNESS

The innocent animal becomes responsible insofar as he is endowed with logos: he has a certain understanding of himself, some knowledge of things, he is placed before various choices, he uses a language. "To live according to physis." What can that mean in terms of the use of language? It does not mean misology: justness does not consist in a refusal of language; insofar as I am a man, I am language. Justness consists in a just use of language. Language should be used according to nature, that is to say, to the extent that I can know and understand—and nothing further.

Now, I do not create the language that I use *ex nihilo;* and this language does not correspond to my body. It comes to me completely ready made, and it comes to me in disproportion. It comes to me disproportionate and unjust because latent within it are the results of experiences that are not my own, and it comes to me disproportionate in a more fundamental manner. It surpasses not only my own past and possible experience, it goes beyond any past and possible experience and beyond the sum of all past and possible experiences as well. The language which reaches me ready made does not express my just accord with physis and it does not express the just accord between humanity and physis (assuming that this portion of the sentence is not meaningless). Language which comes to me ready made is not merely logos, it is mythos. For it translates, or better it *is* formal society, theatrical society, antiphysis. It is not merely the language of knowing and comprehending: it is the language of belief. It assumes a sort of autonomous theatrical existence, fascinating and deceptive: it is collective myth, and the substance of all our collective myths. Public language necessarily is a language of publicity.

The ready-made language which society proposes to me or imposes upon me masks as much as it points out its own nature. And when in fascination I use it, or when I am used by it, I mask what I say and I mask myself: I become a social person, a theatrical persona. How does one, starting with this unjust language, strive toward justness? There is the philosophical method, which claims to supersede all other ways. There is the group of scientific languages. I would like here to point out two other methods.

The first (historically the second) is what I shall call the romantic way, and which could also be called the poetic method: it is by progressing from romanticism that poetry achieves its autonomy. It serves to transfigure the mythic power which social language carries along with itself. Instead of being fascinated by this power, drowned in it, the poet masters it and uses it for his own ends. For he has sensed in the disproportion of social language an instrument for verbally realizing the infinite meaning he subjectively is, for revealing the subjective mystery. On the one hand, social language is excessive in relation to reality; on the other, romantic subjectivity is excessive in comparison to any object. The poet redeems the unjustness of social language in poetic justice. The collective myth is shattered and in its place poetic myth arises. This poetic myth is just, this mythos is logos, for it is no longer designed for belief, for hypnotism, but rather for fidelity to the subjective. What used to be the vehicle for collective belief becomes the expression of self-comprehension. What was a mask of both the objective and the subjective, of the real and of the ideal, becomes a realization of subjectivity.

The other method aims at a reduction. One attempts to eliminate what is excessive in theatrical language, the nests of belief, in order to limit himself to the indication of what is actually known and of self-comprehension as a knowing consciousness (no longer as a poetic subjectivity). This method is not concerned with self-realization *in* language, but with designation and self-designation by means of language. This is the method chosen by Meursault in accordance with his temperament.

These two methods could probably be called "the subjective" and "the objective." We could speak, in order to simplify things, of Meursault's objectivity, of an adequation he seeks with the object. But the two words "objective" and "subjective" would, in their opposition, be occasions for misunderstanding. It is best to avoid both of them whenever possible.

What I may say at any rate is that the Epicurean virtues of prudence, equity, courage, and justness are well illustrated by the use which Meursault makes of language.

The narrative opens with these sentences: "My mother died today. Or maybe yesterday, I don't know. I received a telegram from the home: 'Your mother deceased. Rites tomorrow. Yours sincerely.' That doesn't mean anything. Maybe it was yesterday."

Throughout his narration, Meursault appears to take pains, as here, to avoid saying things he does not know, even when speaking of details which hardly seem to matter. It is important to him to define the limits of what he knows. In noting the facts themselves, he attempts to be as complete as possible. But when memory fails him, he says as much: he does not fabulate. Likewise he says that he does not understand something if he does not understand it, without attempting to invent gratuitous interpretations or to supply ready-made explanations: "From the strange little sound that crossed the partition, I understood that he was weeping. I have no idea why that brought my mother to mind." He takes care to correct a snap judgment, even if such correction adds nothing to his narrative: "I even had the feeling that the corpse lying there among them all meant nothing to them. But I think, now, that it was a false impression." He does not unthinkingly subscribe to ready-made opinions.

Thus, considering his neighbor and his dog: "Celeste said that it was 'quite unfortunate' but of course nobody can tell."

An expression recurring within Meursault's narrative marks his punctilious regard for justness and accuracy. It is the expression "in a sense," a familiar enough expression but one which Meursault enhances by using it in rather unexpected moments. For example:

"He said that time was passing very quickly and, in a sense, that was true. . . . In a sense, that threw me off balance. But, in another, it was killing time. . . . It was, in a sense, an advantage. . . . In a sense, it was interesting to watch a trial. . . . It followed, annoyingly enough, that a condemned man had to wish for a proper functioning of the machine. I say that that was the defective side of things. It is true, in a sense. But in another sense, I was obliged to recognize that the whole secret of a good organization was there. I concluded that a condemned man was obliged to collaborate morally."

Meursault restricts himself to noting what was clearly evident to him, physically and psychologically.

He devotes a great part of his narrative, almost the entire first phase, to presenting concrete phenomena in their proper succession. He shows himself to be precise, and he attempts to accord each remembered phenomenon equal importance. Of course he makes cuts in his past: he does not record, for instance, his working day at the office. But when he attempts to describe, for example, an evening with a friend, he informs us of the most trifling events: "We went out and Raymond offered me a brandy. Then he wanted to play some billiards, and I just barely lost." Each of the phenomena he remembered has its equal right, one might say, to verbal exposure.

Though it is neither lyric nor epic, Meursault's narrative does not adopt the arid tone of a report. Meursault presents phenomena as they appeared to him by informing implicitly or explicitly about his reaction, and interrupts to make corrective observations if his initial reaction now seems inappropriate. Let us quote a passage which gives the general tone:

"I did not hear the woman's name, and I understood only that she was the nurse on duty. She unsmilingly lowered her long, bony face. Then we stood out of the way in order to let the body go past. We followed the pallbearers and went out of the home. The car was in front of the door. Varnished, oblong and glowing, the car resembled a pencil box. Beside it was the director, a little man in ridiculous clothing, with an old man who had a self-conscious way about him."

The way in which Meursault presents psychological phenomena is reminiscent of the simple and even simplistic psychology that surprises us in the ancient philosophers. One does not find complexity in them, the multiplicity of planes illustrated in modern psychological fiction. For them, subjectivity is not distinct from objectivity, it is not allowed to develop its own dimensions. The psychological is treated on a single plane, flush with the physical, in direct contact with the concrete.

45

This way of treating psychology reflects Meursault's temperament, and is in harmony with it; but it is dictated also by his punctilious care not to allow himself to be led astray by an excess of language: "One must not exaggerate," he says. And, following a popular understatement, he consistently labels as bothersome or boring anything which risks troubling his ataraxia.

The psychological vocabulary that we find in social language, with its categories and values, is a good example of the theatricality of that language. The sentiments it orchestrates are conditioned reflexes, collective myths. Society furnishes our sensibilities roles to play, costumes in which our sensibility may make itself decently recognizable on stage. By choosing a poetic method I can shatter this hardened inauthenticity, this hypocrisy in the etymological sense of the word. By being constructively faithful to inspiration, I disengage from the sentimental Tables. Instead of imposing ready-made costumes upon my sensibility, I give it form and realize it in language. Meursault chooses another method. He isolates emotion in the moment, he attaches it to a place. He does not speak of sentiments, but of tastes and dislikes.

The result is a flat psychological language. Meursault's simple explanations, which often seem superfluous, may be contrasted with the explanations of Proust. In particular there is Meursault's use of the conjunction "because." Here are examples:

"After several months she would have cried if they had taken her out of the home. Still because of habit. That is partly the reason why during the last

46

year I hardly ever went there. And also because that would have taken my Sunday away. . . . I fried some eggs and I ate them right out of the pan without any bread because I had none left and because I didn't want to go out and buy some. . . . I turned my chair around and arranged it like the tobacco-merchant's because I found that that way was more comfortable. . . . I slept a bit because I had drunk too much wine. . . . I smoked Raymond's cigarettes because I had none left. . . . I needed her very much because she had on a dress with red and white stripes, and leather sandals. . . . Then he wanted to go to a bordello, but I said no because I don't like them. . . . Then I did not pay any more attention to this tic because I was too busy feeling how much good the sunlight was doing me. . . . To tell the truth, I had not followed his line of reasoning very well, at first because I was hot and there were huge flies in his office that kept lighting on my body, and then again because he frightened me a bit. I realized at the same time that that was ridiculous because, after all, I was the criminal."

The rejection of theatrical structures in his spontaneous life and in his elaborated life produces a sort of psychophysical phenomenism appropriate to the Epicurean conception of physis. Phenomena, sentences follow one another, but they are not allied, remain unorganized. Subordination and even coordination are avoided except in the case of brief reasonings. Meursault's knowing consciousness scarcely gathers things together: it respects the individuality of a phenomenon.

47

However, these remarks lose some of their accuracy as one approaches the conclusion of the narrative: Meursault's reasonings little by little encroach upon descriptions. In prison, and especially after sentencing, Meursault attempts to take himself in hand, to gather his life together. Then one rediscovers the original meaning of *legein:* to assemble.

In his verbal relationships with people, Meursault applies the rule, "Overdo nothing." He is taciturn and discreet. He attempts to maintain language in the indicative and he would like other people to do the same. His language is utilitarian and descriptive: Meursault is a positivist. He attaches a moral value to such a use of language: his taciturnity and discretion are a modesty. Thus in the course of an interview with his lawyer:

"He asked me if I had felt grief that day. That question astonished me, and it seemed to me that I would have been very embarrassed if I had had to ask it."

He dislikes curiosity animated by the desire for something other than knowledge and intellection. He dislikes intersubjective relationships that overleap the bounds of work or of a shared game. He dislikes searching for a communion that would be more than cooperation. For all these would be unnatural and unnecessary desires, all theatrical: they rely upon a theatrical use of language. "One should never play," he says, meaning a comedian's acting by "play." The "moral" judgments with which men attempt to weigh down one another in their constant pursuit of scapegoats rely upon the theatrical use of language. With these, Meursault is not only uncomfortable, he does not understand.

He is told that the people in his neighborhood judged him adversely when he committed his mother to an old peoples' home. He remarks: "I answered, though I still don't know why, that I had no idea until now that people had judged me that way, but that the home seemed a natural choice to me since I didn't have enough money to have Mother taken care of."

Similarly, the theatrical use which the prosecutor makes of his lack of repentance astonishes him: "At that moment, he turned toward me and pointed his finger at me and continued to heap abuses without my really understanding why. True, I could not prevent myself from realizing that he was right. I was not regretful of my act. But his relentlessness astonished me."

On the other hand, Meursault understands and approves a just use of language practiced by others, even when it is disadvantageous for him. The passage just cited contains one example. Others:

"It was true, and I knew it. . . . He appeared very reasonable and rather nice. . . . I thought that his way of seeing things was not lacking in clarity. What he was saying seemed plausible. . . . That appeared evident, and I fell in with his reasoning. . . . Coldly considering things, it was completely natural."

The attitude of detached impartiality that he adopts is what he expects from others. Interrogated by the examining magistrate or by the presiding judge, he answers as though he were participating in a test: "He only asked me in the same somewhat tired manner if I regretted my act. I reflected on that, and answered that, more than true regret, I felt a certain boredom."

This attitude cannot always be imputed to simple naïveté. There is courage when, asked by the Arab prisoners about what crime he has committed, Meursault responds that he has killed an Arab.

The moment that his scruple for accuracy appears most clearly as moral, voluntary, and systematic is probably when the lawyer asks Meursault, if not to put a false face on concrete facts, at least to pretend to have experienced a good deal of grief at his mother's funeral. Meursault answers that he cannot do so "because it is false." And he remarks: "He looked at me strangely, as if someway I disgusted him."

This love of justness, allied to his innocence, will make Meursault a stranger to theatrical society. Frankness, impartiality, modesty, courage: Meursault's narration reaches a sovereign dignity. This dignity is strange, it is foreign to theatrical society. This dignity of an animal possessing language is in opposition to the hypocrisy of the social comedian and disturbs this society. It is in essentially those terms that Meursault will be adjudged guilty.

CHAPTER 4

GUILT

Meursault walks along the beach for the third time. The first time he was with two friends, the second with one. Now, he is alone. The sunlight blinds him, the heat stifles him, he cannot bear the glare from the sea and the sand: "I stood up very straight in order to overcome the opaque drunkenness the sun poured into me." He could go back to the cabin where the women are, but he does not wish to approach them. Allied with the sun, both the earth and the sea seem to repel him, or to smother him. But there is a spring. Meursault walks toward it.

The path to the spring is blocked by one of the Arabs whom Meursault's friends had come up against during their first walk along the beach. Meursault approaches. The Arab takes out his knife. Meursault draws the revolver one friend had entrusted to him.

"Then everything lurched. The sea sent forth a thick and burning breath. It seemed to me that the sky was opening up for a rain of fire."

Meursault fires.

"I understood that I had destroyed the day's balance, the extraordinary silence of a beach where I had been happy. Then I fired again, four times, at the inert body. The bullets hammered at it without making a mark. And it was as though with four short blows I was striking against the door of misfortune."

Before examining how Meursault's act will be interpreted according to the myths and rites of theatrical society, it is advisable to see how he interprets it himself.

First, he does not consider it, properly speaking, as an act. Rather, he considers it as an event, as a fact, as something that has happened or something he witnessed. It is a certain phenomenon of which he is aware. Meursault's consciousness remains in its role of cognitive awareness, the role of a witnessing consciousness.

He will be asked the reason for his act. This question is meant to attract Meursault into the sphere of the human and theatrical. The city wishes to extract a motive that would explain the act, that would account for it as the manifestation of a human agent, more precisely as the gesture of a dramatic persona. His action has resulted in the death of a person, of a character. The murder of a character must be accounted for as a motive of a dramatic character. Meursault's action must be extracted from the realm of things that happen in order to take its place and receive judgment on the stage of a tribunal. The judge implies this to a witness who states that the whole affair is a "misfortune": "Yes, we know. But we are here to judge misfortunes of precisely this nature."

Interrogated on the reasons for his action, Meursault can answer only: "It was because of the sun." Making use of his flat psychology, he reduces the psychomoral to the psychophysical. He attempts to give a "natural" explanation (employing one of his favorite words) because for him it is the only valid type of explanation. He could not bear the brightness of the sunlight and the weight of the heat; he was going toward a spring to find relief; an obstacle was present, he brought it down. Instead of the motive that society wishes him to present, he suggests a cause. This might do in a scientific discussion, but it will not suffice in a theatrical production.

However, there is a resonance in the words used by Meursault to describe the episode on the beach, a resonance to which Meursault's previous narrative has not accustomed us. Meursault is no longer in the presence of particular objects, but in the presence of the elements themselves: he is overwhelmed, possessed by elemental powers, by the power of that solar fire that impregnates not only the air but also the earth and the sea. The sun pours an "opaque drunkenness" into him.

Physis here is alien and terrifying in its domination. In order to discuss the resonance revealed in Meursault's account, in order to furnish images for this sensation of the overwhelming, we are tempted to deify the natural, to pass from an Ionian to a tragic vision, from a concrete to a mythological language. When Meursault says, "It was because of the sun," we are reminded of Orestes and wish to say, as in *The Eumenides*, "It was because of Loxias." True, the sun is not presented as a god in Meursault's account, but a deification is suggested. The sun pursues Meursault from the beginning of the narrative: "the sun was the same as on the day I buried Mother." And when Meursault remarks, "I thought I only had to turn back and it would all be over, but the whole beach pulsing with the sun pressed up behind me," we may imagine Orestes compelled along the road to Argos by Delphic Apollo.

In *The Eumenides* Orestes is judged by a human tribunal. A good part of the crime being attributed to Apollo, the jury divides evenly, and Orestes is acquitted by Athena's vote. In this instance, we attend a triumph of the theatre: the theatre triumphs in a play that takes place at the tribunal. The theatrical has absorbed the natural and it has even absorbed the sacred: in a way Apollo is judged, Athena adds her vote to that of the jurors, the Furies are appeased. Nothing of this sort occurs in *The Stranger*. The theatre does not manage to digest the rest for two reasons.

The first reason is that, unlike Orestes' crime, Meursault's will not be "swallowed" as a crime of passion. In the French version of the judicial comedy, a crime of passion is granted extenuating circumstances, but this label refers above all to crimes inspired by jealous love, those crimes about which it can be said, "It was because of Aphrodite." Unlike Apollo, Aphrodite has retained her right to citizenship because without her the theatre of human relations would lose much of its spark. One thus pardons, in her honor, those accused who lay claim to her. But it could hardly be the same for an accused who appeals the sun. The sun has too regular a course, it is too natural and too remote; despite its occasional Miles Gloriosus aspect, the sun does not manifest an authentically theatrical disposition. Theatrical "justice" cannot stomach a solar motive. When someone kills because of Aphrodite, it is definitely a person he wishes to kill. But Meursault, who kills "because of the sun," wished only to remove an obstacle from the road to the spring, perhaps not even that.

Moreover, and this is the second reason, Meursault himself does not present his act as a crime of passion: he does not plead his solar drunkenness as an excuse, but as an explanation. He does not say, "It is the fault of the sun (Apollo)"; he says, "It was because of the sun." Nor does this explanation have a deterministic character. Meursault stresses that he was not in a dazed condition: "I thought I only had to turn back and it would all be over," and somewhat later, "Because of this scalding, which I could stand no longer, I moved forward. I knew it was stupid, that I could not get rid of the sun by moving one step, but I took a step, only one step forward."

On the other hand, if Meursault does not offer excuses, neither does he accuse himself. He says what happened, he tells the circumstances, he makes his report. He does not assume moral responsibility any more than he rejects it, or at least, he does not understand moral responsibility in the same sense as his judges understand it. Assuming responsibility, as his judges see it, is to assume it after the fact while facing the tribunal: and assuming this responsibility properly consists in making a show of repentance. For Meursault, responsibility has not this theatrical quality. In his own eyes, he is responsible before himself during the act: this means simply that he must choose to do one thing or another. He cannot be responsible after the fact, since he cannot change what has been done. After the fact his responsibility to himself and, accessorily, to others consists in correctly using language to tell what has happened. No doubt, Meursault may not merely describe, he may also interpret and, thus, judge. He can recognize that he has erred, but this means that he has committed an error, not a "sin."

At the moment of the crime, Meursault realizes and attempts to interpret his error: "I understood that I had destroyed the day's balance." This expression resonates in us, evoking classical reminiscences, and again we are tempted to extrapolate. Day's balance. We recall in *Le Cimetière marin*, "Noon the just . . . O my silence!" And again:

> L'âme exposée aux torches du solstice
> Je te soutiens, admirable justice
> De la lumière aux armes sans pitié!

Meursault's body could not sustain the "admirable justice of a pitiless armed light." Symbolically, and noisily, he has broken the order of physis: *dike.* Properly speaking, he has not broken this order by arrogating the right to administer death. He does not feel this power: the Arab is nothing more than an obstacle on the path to a spring. More simply, he has broken the order by introducing the use of an artificial object—the revolver—into a natural plenitude. *Tekne* has been exercised immoderately. Meursault's error is felt as an aesthetic fault. This is implied by the use of the word "balance" and by what follows: "I understood that I had destroyed the day's balance, the extraordinary silence of a beach where I had been happy."

It seems that at this point we might give way to temptation. We have seen already that concrete aesthetic values were important to Meursault, that his sensuality had a strong aesthetic bent. The happiness he found at the beach had an aesthetic quality. The expression "where I had been happy" perhaps adds a shading of a feeling of ingratitude. But this hypothesis is somewhat gratuitous, and it is probably best to be content with seeing here the preparation of a contrast with the word "misfortune" that ends the passage. Meursault's error was also to have broken away in one gesture from a naturally happy life.

An aesthetic interpretation of his crime encounters one small difficulty. Let us examine the difficulty and see if we cannot eliminate it. The "noon" in which Meursault commits his error was not described to us as "just." The light blinds Meursault, the heat stifles him. From this point of view, Meursault's gesture appears in harmony with the disproportionateness of the sun. I am led, in consequence, to state a distinction between the pleasing and the beautiful. Generally speaking, the two have been united in Meursault's experience. Yet concerning light, the narrative has already pointed out both a "purity" of light "injurious to the eyes" (the light in question being admittedly artificial) and, the morning of the funeral, "the brimming sun that made the countryside shudder, making it inhuman and depressing." The sun's splendor may be felt as both beautiful and disagreeable, possibly unbearable. Beauty in its luminous purity can hold something terrible. More generally, beauty may be said to be inhuman. Walking along the beach, Meursault feels only the unpleasant aspect of the solar dominion. He feels, to employ Heraclitean terminology, that the sun is overreaching its bounds. But it is perhaps even more the case, still employing the same terminology, that Meursault's psyche is too "humid." The echo of the first pistol shot reveals to him that he has broken the silent splendor, a radiance which during the first part of the morning had provided him with a flawless joy.

The last lines of the chapter remain to be interpreted. "Then I fired again, four times, at the inert body. The bullets hammered at it without making a mark. And it was as if with four short blows I was striking against the door of misfortune."

The connection with what precedes is assured by the passage from the word "happy" to "misfortune." The meaning is enlarged, and driven home. With his first shot, Meursault has broken the aesthetic balance of the setting and he has broken with the happiness that was his in this place. With the four additional shots, Meursault intensifies and expands the import of his error. What once counted only because of a given place and moment now counts for a lifetime.

This, at least, is how he seems to feel. He has broken not only the balance of the day, but also the equilibrium of his own days; he has broken away from his own spontaneous happiness in life. He beats against the door of misfortune, that is, against the gates of a prison. And doubtless he had already obligated himself to prison and condemnation with the first pistol shot. But he does not seem to have felt that; besides, those four shots would aggravate his case in men's eyes.

Considering those additional shots, Meursault feels that he is placing himself in disharmony with the laws of the city, with *nomos* and not with *dike* alone. This does not mean that he feels guilty in the sense the judges will attempt to instill in him. Here again, he escapes the theatrical sphere. For the law as it stands is part of the natural milieu in which Meursault lives. Law is an object of knowledge. Meursault knows that he is "doing something stupid." He does not feel guilty, yet he realizes that he is a criminal; he knows that he is placing himself within the sphere of enforcement of penal law. That is the attitude he will maintain during his trial. He once was free, and worked in an office; he will become a prisoner and a criminal.

May we ask why he took those additional four shots? This is the question asked by the district attorney, and Meursault cannot answer it. Is it legitimate then to attempt formulating an answer? At any rate, it will be better to present the answer as an hypothesis, and in the "as if" form.

We have seen what the four shots entail for

Meursault. Did he *wish* for it to happen? For support, we have only the end of a sentence, "as if with four short blows I was striking against the door of misfortune." Might we interpret the verb "to strike" with all its active force? Meursault would call for misfortune, he would wish to enter into unhappiness, to hammer down upon himself the consequences of his error. It would be as though Meursault perversely wished to be punished for having destroyed "the day's balance," as though he wished to remove an impious flaw, himself, from the beach, from the radiance he defiled, to remove this human stain from the beach and yield it up to its peers, men like himself, as though he wished to take upon himself the ugliness he has introduced.

But I am giving way to the temptation of psychoanalysis, and by so doing I am no longer faithful to Meursault, to his actual reporting, or to the personality he reveals. I have tried to determine what the first shot and the four that follow signify for Meursault; in attempting to go further, I risk overreaching.

The apparatus of the law demarcates a certain social order and defines the means of protecting it. In principle, application of the law thus is presented as a pragmatic and technical activity, not as a set of theatrical gestures. But in fact, it is not merely said that the law is applied, it is said that "justice" is meted out. The social order is consecrated into a moral order. The criminal is not taken merely for what he is: someone who has placed himself in the field of the application of penal law. The criminal, especially a murderer, is conceived of as someone who has infringed a moral law.

Now, properly speaking, there is no moral law, or at least moral law cannot be seen from that perspective. Morality is born with each individual endowed with intelligence who experiences choice. It is developed through the range of intelligence and through opportunities for choice. If there is a moral law, it is what that individual invents in harmony with his experience and comprehension. Only this law can properly be termed "moral," for it alone can be just. Of course, I may notice coincidences between the moral law which I formulate according to my sensitive and intellectual nature and the laws of the city. But then the law of the city is not moral because it is the law of the city; it is moral to the extent that my judgment confers it morality.

But often the inverse process is encountered. I may consider that a certain act is moral so far as it accords with the law (either written or law of opinion). I may consider the law of the city as moral a priori. This is possible if I blind myself, if I am hypnotized, it is possible through self-hypocrisy. I refuse to understand what is occurring within myself, I thrust myself into belief.

If there is a duty dictated by my nature, it is the duty of making for myself a morality as far as my intelligence and my experience of choice permit. To consecrate the laws of the city as moral a priori is to avoid the way to self-comprehension and to thrust myself into the slough of belief, substituting for myself a theatrical character that conforms to the law:

this is immorality itself. It is, however, to this fundamental immorality that the name of morality is cus-
tomarily given. How does one live within this contra-
diction?

There is a kind of somnambulism, and this
somnambulism rests upon intellectual inertia, my
own and that of other people. The continuance of my
self-hypocrisy is dependent upon hypocrisy around
me. A belief which does not feel universal feels itself
in danger. The criminal can endanger this kind of
belief.

If I understand the law for what it is, the penalty
imposed upon a criminal appears designed to prevent
a man from endangering the wellbeing and the existence of citizens. It relies, rightly or wrongly, on the
empirical psychological principle according to which
someone who has done something once will most
likely do it again; and it relies also upon another
empirical principle which grants an educational value
to example: the penalty will cause both the criminal
and the innocent to reflect. It is not a matter of chas-
tising the criminal, it is a matter of preventing him
from harming others. But as soon as one speaks of
chastisement, of punishment, it is no longer the existence or the wellbeing of citizens one wishes to
protect, it is their hypocrisy. Criminal defiance might
bring us out of our hypocrisy. We will be grateful
to the criminal who makes a show of repentance: true,
this does not bring him back into the legal order, but
it causes him to re-enter the moral order, and this
pacifies us.

This way of conceiving morality, or rather of

spiriting away morality, may be called religious. The theatre which takes itself seriously, which does not wish to admit its theatricality, may be termed religious. Two of the three characters representing theatrical society in Meursault's narrative call themselves Christian, and a third suggests it. It is fitting here to recall the "Christian" schema that was set up, to see its connection with the hypocritical manner of conceiving morality and the substitution of law for morality. Being immoderate language, any religion may be called theatrical; but the religion of "my" Christian, being very "human," is the more theatrical.

I remark first that through its antiphysical nature the "Christian" schema offers a privileged position to the theatre. The Divine City is a society of souls: what is natural within and around men has been eliminated; things which furnish human space-time have disappeared. "The theatre," said Mallarmé, "is an absolute place."

Only human souls can belong to the society of the chosen: only men, being capable of language, are capable of theatre. And then again not all men. There is a selection, a judgment, a tribunal where a human persona is judged by a divine persona. I pointed out a nontheatrical element in the application of social law, a technical and pragmatic element: one seeks to protect the wellbeing and the lives of citizens. Contrarily, the application of divine law is purely theatrical: it cannot concern, in fact, the protection of anything whatsoever. A criminal soul cannot menace elect souls, cannot menace their wellbeing or their lives, cannot provide them a bad example. The concern then is to chasten and to punish, and nothing else. I have called this unpragmatic aspect of social law "religious."

Which souls are recognized as guilty? Those that have lacked belief, that have practiced neither virtue nor repentance. Belief dominates and extends beyond the other two terms. It extends beyond them, for, among articles of faith there are propositions having no ethical application. It dominates them because virtue and repentance have no meaning except through belief. A virtue is virtuous not because human intelligence has decided it so, but because it was so commanded by divine law. Divine law is, a priori, moral. To be virtuous, one thus must believe that a proposed law to be found in books or on certain lips is of divine origin, hence moral. It is not a matter of understanding in order to judge, it is a case of believing in order to consecrate. This is shown well enough by the fact that repentance can be as efficacious, and even more efficacious, than virtue. Repentance is efficacious even at the last instant, that is to say when all further practice of virtue is denied. Repentance can be efficacious because it manifests belief, the unpragmatic and theatrical recognition of divine law as moral a priori. Beating his chest, the publican acknowledges the moral order of the Pharisee, and that is all the Pharisee asks. My Christian is at once both publican and Pharisee. He combines the two attitudes: fundamentally, they amount to the same thing.

This resemblance between a religious attitude and a social ceremony, a resemblance founded in the essential nature of the theatre, unifies what Meursault comes up against in the second half of the narrative. The theatre excludes him and one may say that it is justice because Meursault wished to exclude the theatrical from himself. In his last moments, he will realize the justice of his fate. For it is just that a just man, by being just, be rejected by injustice.

Let us analyze the forms under which injustice, disproportionateness, hypocrisy, and belief loom before Meursault.

First, there is the examining magistrate. It happens that this curious character not only considers himself a Christian but that he also mixes religion with the exercise of his functions:

"He told me rapidly and with passion that he believed in God, that conviction told him that no man was too guilty for God not to forgive him, though it was necessary for a man by repentance to become like a little child again, whose soul is empty and ready to accept anything."

This comparison is amusing because it depicts Meursault rather well, even though the examining magistrate sees Meursault as a "hardened soul." In fact this believer is not at all interested in spontaneity and innocence; he is interested in a child only as catechumen. Despite what he says, he is interested in a soul prepared not to welcome anything, but ready to welcome what he wants that soul to welcome. But why is this believer so interested in the repentance of others? The connection between belief and the desire that others repent appears in a clear, indeed caricatural, manner some lines further. Meursault has just confessed that he does not believe in God:

"He told me that it was impossible, that all men believed in God, even those who were turning away from His face. This was his belief, and if he should ever doubt it, his life would no longer make sense. 'Do you want,' he exclaimed, 'my life to mean nothing?' I thought that was none of my business, and told him so. But across the table he was already thrusting the crucifix under my eyes and was shouting in an unreasonable fashion, 'Don't you see, I'm a Christian. I beg forgiveness for your sins through Christ here. How can you keep from believing that He suffered for you?'"

The fact that someone does not believe can appear scandalous and dangerous to the believer. A belief which does not feel universal feels itself endangered. The simple fact that Meursault states his disbelief in the magistrate's God gives the latter the impression that his life is losing its meaning.

In fact, the examining magistrate does not rely upon the meaning which his life could be for him. He has misunderstood, or has refused to understand the relation between "meaning" and "life." My life has no meaning, it cannot have any meaning because it *is* meaning, because it provides meanings and values. But a believer feigns finding meaning outside of himself in the theatre where he is a character. The collective myth is supposed to give meaning to life, as though a label could give wine its savor. In fact, it is sensibility alone that may give sense, or significance, to the collective myth, to a formless heap of

words and gestures. A believer hides from this relation, he reverses it. He conceals himself as meaning
by adopting a mask, by becoming a persona. But the
solidity of that mask and the stability of that persona
are dependent upon the gestures and words of other
characters, since it is from the exterior that meaning
is presumed to come. A character like Meursault who
plays his role badly, who is in the audience and in
the wings as well as on stage (does he not say when
speaking of his own trial that he would like to "witness" a trial?) endangers the fiction of believers.

I prefer potatoes to carrots; I meet someone who
prefers carrots to potatoes; that does not make me
uneasy. Similarly, my sensibility may be of the type
that finds images in the Christian myth that are suited
to it: I may have a Christian sensibility, one which
gives a value to the images of the Christian myth. If
I am aware of that, comprehend it and hold myself
justly to it, meeting a pagan temperament could not
disturb me any more than meeting an enthusiast of
carrots. But that is because I adopt a just attitude
toward those images, a poetic attitude, not the religious attitude of belief.

The believer *per se,* if he meets an unbeliever, is
inclined to turn into an exhibitionist: "I am a Christian." (That seems to imply, "I am not myself." But
the implication is rather, "I am more than myself.")
He is likewise apt to turn into a missionary: because
the meaning of his life is supposed to come from the
exterior, he must attempt to erase the stain that has
just appeared in the field which diffuses "meaning."
Such a believer becomes a tyrant. His tyranny may

be mild but it is extreme, because it claims domination not only over the actions of others but over their thoughts and even their sensibilities as well. The believer wishes to erase nature itself in its spontaneous generation in others, in order to avoid sensing that he has stifled it in himself.

It can be said that the myth of my Christian makes theatre out of the sentiment of the divine and the sacred. The judicial theatre, on the other hand, consecrates characters: it makes allegories out of them. There are the defense, the jury, the prosecution, and the law; instead of a man who is accused and others who pursue the professions of lawyer, prosecutor, or judge, or the fortuitous and temporary occupation of juror.

"The defense, that was myself," says Meursault. But it is also his lawyer who, in his speech, takes his allegorical role seriously. He says "I," thus placing himself in his client's place as did the Athenian logographers (but in that case, at least, it was the accused who read the speech). The part of the public that is publication and publicity is also allegorized. Meursault asks who those men are. He is told that they are "the Press." Jurors do not appear as particular living individuals. Essentially, they are the group:

"It was then that I saw a row of faces before me. They were all looking at me: I understood that that was the jury. But I can't say what distinguished any of them from the others. I had only one impression: I was in front of a tramway bench and all the anonymous travelers were looking over a new arrival in order to pick out the ridiculous things about him."

The substitution of a collective persona for living individuals is not due merely to technical organization. The pragmatic and industrial value of this substitution is surpassed: the substitution acquires a magic value, there is a consecration. Meursault himself becomes sacred in his role of scapegoat. And the formula of condemnation is not content with ruling over the fate of Meursault "in conformity with the law": Meursault will be "beheaded in a public place in the name of the French People." Mentioning the people instead of the law marks consecration. "The law" may pass for a technical and pragmatic term, but not "the People." It is not by means of a popular referendum that Meursault's fate has been decided. "The People" is the people by divine right, the allegorical people of the democratic theatre, the successor of the king by divine right.

From characters, let us proceed to themes. If Meursault has been arrested and if he has been condemned to a punishment, it is doubtlessly because of his act. But if he has been condemned to the penalty of death, it is because he has not made a show of grief conforming to the rules of the theatre during his mother's funeral and in the days that followed, and because now he makes no show of repentance. The gravity of the punishment is due to the fact that Meursault has made no sacrifice to hypocrisy, the concealed goddess of the religious theatre.

From repentance, let us turn to filial love. A certain morality called Christian has consecrated filial devotion. In this sentimental manner of conceiving morality can be found again the religious propensity toward tyranny over not only the actions but also the thoughts and even the sensibilities of other people. Logically, loving or not loving an individual who carries the label of mother or father is neither more nor less moral than liking or disliking potatoes and carrots. What is theatrical in this filial piety is easily disclosed. The father and mother must be loved not because they may happen to be lovable individuals but because they are the father and the mother, because they are fitted with certain social labels. What is lovable is not an individual as he is, but a phantom, a persona. The irony is that filial love is very often celebrated, and required, as a "natural" sentiment.

The choice of filial love as a reflex for conditioning and for consecrating is not the doing of my Christian alone. Filial love is required by public opinion. Is this choice arbitrary? It seems that basically one encounters the notion that morality consists in obedience, in submitting to the reigning theatre. Before being widely social, the theatrical stage is familial. The father and the mother are intended as the guardians of theatrical morality. A child is supposed to receive his flesh and his spirit alike from his parents, so far as they represent the social theatre. The expression "filial love" would thus seem a smokescreen projected around what is, in fact, of interest: intellectual inertia, obedience to tradition.

Loving or not loving individuals who happen to be one's mother and father theoretically has nothing to do with being a criminal. The official laws of the city are not concerned with that. Yet the theme of filial love will be exploited by the prosecutor, as Meursault's lawyer has warned. Meursault "was fond" of his mother, and he "wishes that she had not died." To which his lawyer responds, "That's not enough."

It is not enough because such phrases are not theatrical enough, they will not reach past the foot-lights. The day of the funeral, Meursault did not demonstrate ostentatious grief. The society upon which Meursault depends is less demanding than my Christian: it pretends to control only words and actions. But with respect to those, at least, society stands firm. Thus the prosecutor zealously exploits Meursault's lack of theatricality which is his basic crime. The amazing rhetoric which can rise from a ceremony intended, in principle, only to apply the law, is well illustrated by the prosecutor:

"Yes, the jury will decide. And they will conclude that a stranger could offer coffee, but that a son had to refuse it before the body of the one who brought him into the world."

Let us concentrate our attention on the character of the prosecutor and upon his words. The prosecutor speaks of his "duty." Under the circumstances, his duty seems to consist in making Meursault's criminality theatrical. But how can he be made theatrical if he is to be condemned for a lack of theatricality? The method is simple: he is presented as a monster. The natural monster is living and, yet, goes counter to the accepted norms of life. Likewise, this theatrical monster appears on stage, yet he goes counter to the accepted rules of the theatre. The theatrical monster disturbs our notion of theatrical order just as a natural monster disturbs our notion of the natural order. He is a scandal. Of course, the prosecutor will not present Meursault as a monster in terms of theatrical order. Serious and religious theatre cannot see itself as theatre without drifting away from hypocrisy into cynicism, which makes theatricality show up clearly. "Being a hypocrite is better than being a cynic," said, if I am not mistaken, the Christian dramatist Claudel. Meursault will be presented by the prosecutor as a monster in terms of the "moral" order, as a "moral monster."

The resemblance of the language of the serious theatre to the religious language of my Christian is observable in the use that the prosecutor makes of the word "soul." Among the possible definitions of the soul of my Christian the following may be chosen: the soul is the manner in which a Christian is supposed to appear before the eyes of his God as judge. Social law itself cannot judge the soul. It is interested solely in certain actions, certain gestures, and in their possible consequences. Yet Meursault is judged not merely for his actions but for his soul as well. The theatre has intervened: for Meursault's soul, according to the prosecutor, is Meursault's persona, a moral monster.

At first the prosecutor says "heart," a word already somewhat mythic and unphysiologically taken: "I accuse this man of having buried his mother with a criminal heart." The criminal is someone who has committed a crime. That has nothing to do with the "heart," and that has especially nothing to do with Meursault at his mother's funeral. In this sentence one observes the manner in which a religious language is formed: a pragmatic and technical language ("criminal" and "buried") is mixed with a sentimental and pseudopoetic language ("a mother" and "a heart").

From "the heart of a criminal" the prosecutor progresses to "a criminal soul":

"He said that he had bent over my soul and that he had found nothing, gentlemen of the jury. He said that in actual fact I had no soul, that there was nothing human about me, and that none of the moral principles which men keep in their hearts was accessible to me. Of course, he went on, we cannot reproach him because of this. We cannot complain that he lacks what he cannot have. But when it becomes the concern of this court, the totally negative virtue of tolerance must be transformed into something less easy, but more elevated—into justice. Especially when a lack of heart such as we discover in this man can grow into an abyss to which society itself can succumb."

The incoherences of this passage arise from the concerns of a theatrical language which, being serious, pretends to be something other than what it is.

The prosecutor says that nothing human is accessible to Meursault. However, shortly thereafter, he calls him "that man." Indeed, it must be recognized that Meursault is a man: the city's law is not applied to jellyfish, or to boulders. Yet again, in order that Meursault be condemned as the prosecutor wishes him to be, one must somehow conclude that he is essentially inhuman. For it is the social theatre that decides of what essential humanity must consist.

The second incoherence concerns the word "jus-

tice." An intellectual judgment by which Meursault
would be understood or by which he would be declared misunderstood would be just. But here it is not
a question either of understanding Meursault or of
confessing a misunderstanding, it is simply a question
of applying a law, which law does not aim at justice
but instead at the protection of citizens and of a certain moral order which is as it is and which could
be otherwise.

The third incoherence underlies the rhetoric of
the last sentence. How could "society" possibly
"succumb" to "the emptiness of a heart"? That cannot be understood with any rigor unless by "society"
one means not only the legal order but the theatrical
order as well, and by "the emptiness of a heart" a
lack or a rejection of theatricality. The sentence, to
satisfy logic, would have to be written: "The lack (or
rejection) of theatricality such as we discover in this
living individual is counter to the order of theatrical
society."

Putting the passage into logical form would suffice
for us to understand it for what it is, to pass from
hypocrisy to cynicism. In the place of "soul" and
"heart" one would say "persona." In place of "justice" one could write "hypocrisy." In the place of
"moral principles" one could write "theatrical principles." Obviously, the prosecutor is unable to per-
form this rewriting for himself.

The remainder of the prosecutor's speech sub-
scribes to the same logic when it is interpreted according to the order of the theatre. Thus he ends up
affirming that Meursault "is also guilty of the murder

which this court must judge tomorrow," to wit, a parricide. Now, Meursault has not murdered his father; he has not even killed his mother. But in the order of the theatre, there is an equivalence between sentiment and act, and in the system of theatrical society there is an identity between factual reality and collective myth. Meursault has killed his mother symbolically, has not made a public sacrifice before the idol of the mother. He has killed the myth of the mother within himself, which is equivalent to killing, in addition, the myth of the father, which is equivalent to killing a father.

Symbolically murdering one's mother is graver than actually killing an Arab. An Arab is scarcely more than a mechanic in the system of the society that judges Meursault. If we combine Meursault's explanation ("because of the sun") and the accusation of the prosecutor, we obtain an unexpected analogy with the words of Apollo in *The Eumenides:* "I am the cause of his mother's murder."

The prosecutor's conclusion—according to which Meursault has nothing to do with "a society whose essential rules he spurns" and thus cannot appeal to the public's human heart "whose elementary reactions he knows nothing about"—becomes logical if theatricality is exposed, rather than adopted. Rejecting theatricality, Meursault has nothing to do with theatrical society. Rejecting the mask, Meursault cannot participate in the society of masks. And since the collective myth has taken the place of nature, since there are no longer living individuals but only masks, whoever rejects mask and myth reduces himself to zero. Punishing him by death is nothing other than a rite that consecrates what has already been established.

With the chaplain's visit, we are present at the intervention of the strictly religious theatre. On the whole, the chaplain attempts to practice a mild form of religious tyranny, a paternalistic form. Here it is no longer a question of condemning Meursault, but of tempting him, of attempting to retrieve him.

Meursault says to the priest that the subject of the Christian God does not interest him. The priest then asks if he is not speaking in this manner "through an excess of despair." A believer can scarcely admit that his God, the being that in principle interests him most, does not interest other men. That there may be men who do not partake in the hypnosis of the believer can be bothersome enough for him. More irritating yet is that there are men who are not interested, for lack of interest is the surest negation of a value which the believer would wish fundamental and universal.

The priest approaches the subject of sin:

"He was telling me of his certainty that my appeal would be granted, but that I was carrying about the weight of a sin which I must unload. According to him, the justice of men was nothing, and the justice of God everything. I remarked that it was the first that had condemned me. He answered that that had not by any means cleansed my sin. I told him I did not know what a sin was."

The word "criminal," as we have seen it used, was ambiguous. The word had a legal meaning, and a religious connotation. The word "sin" itself has a purely religious meaning. It is the notion of sin that provides the religious connotation of "criminal." With the notion of sin, we are in pure theatre. The sinner is not defined as someone who does evil to someone else or who has infringed social law; he is someone who infringes divine law, someone, it is tempting to say, who does evil to God. But, by definition, no evil whatsoever can be done to God. Instead, the sinner is someone who does evil to his own soul. The fault here is purely mythic. The end of the cited passage shows how Meursault cuts short the chaplain's attempt to tempt him. Meursault reduces the notion of sin to what it is, to something verbal, by stating that he does not know what the word means.

The priest then turns toward a more concrete language, toward a pseudopoetic language:

"All these stones sweat misery, I know. I've never looked at them without anguish. But, from the bottom of my heart, I know that the most miserable among you have seen a divine face emerge from their obscurity. It is this face that we are asking you to see."

Having failed on the sensibility and the intelligence of Meursault, the priest attacks his imagination. The use of the word "we," at once modest and imperative, is of note here. The priest does not speak in propria persona as a living particular individual, but he represents a collective myth and hides in it. "We," the collective myth, asks of Meursault to see a "divine face." For the Christian God does not disdain anthropomorphy. But what could this face which does not correspond to the face of any particular living individual be, other than a theatrical mask, like the character of God-as-judge? Here again, Meursault pricks the rhetorical balloon. If he attempted to imagine a face, it was the face of a particular living individual (that of Marie). Only in this context, outside poetry, may the word "face" be properly employed.

The priest, though, cannot accept defeat. Being unable to win Meursault, he acts as though he had won him. Whether Meursault likes it or not, to the priest he is a creature of the Christian God. Being unable to appropriate Meursault in reality, the being that Meursault is to himself, the priest appropriates his mythic reality, Meursault's persona as creature. To do that the priest has only to consider Meursault, whether the latter likes it or not, as his fellow-being. If he is not recoverable as a repentant sinner, at least Meursault is salvageable a priori as a creature of God, as a fellow-being. This paternalistic tyranny will be exercised in the unreal:

"'No, my son,' he said placing his hand on my shoulder. 'I am always with you. But you cannot know that because your heart has been blinded. I shall pray for you.'"

The theatre has condemned Meursault, then has tempted him. His encounters with the theatre test him. He finds in them the occasion to take on an explicit and total awareness of his implicit philosophy of life. Innocent and just, declared guilty, rejected into solitude, and tempted in the face of death, Meursault will go on to triumph over this testing in order to become a hero.

CHAPTER 5

THE HERO

It has been shown how Meursault attempted to adjust to his condition of prisoner and how, on the other hand, he interpreted his criminal act at the time of its occurrence. Let us now examine his reaction to the theatrical situation made for him, the situation of being a guilty man.

The writing in the first part of the narrative is confident and clear. It is not so in the second half. The tone wavers, there are dissonances. Meursault experiences difficulty in maintaining his positivistic and naturalistic point of view. This wavering, these dissonances suggest the psychological testing through which Meursault passes. He hardly knows how to react to the intervention of the theatre and of the collective myth. For example, at first he adopts a detached attitude about his trial: it would interest him to attend a trial. Then he seems to revolt against the fact that very little consideration is taken of him during court procedures: he is present as a thing. Finally, he recovers his detachment from what is occurring, his mind wanders from the trial, and he would like to be over with it.

He refuses to be absorbed by the theatre, yet since he is the narrator he makes us feel the theatricality of that theatre, and that implies a certain comprehension on his part even though, otherwise, he feigns misunderstanding. We find sentences in his narrative written in the manner of the humorist or the ironist, who feign naïveté and astonishment though they comprehend very well what is going on. Thus when Meursault reports the words of the prosecutor concerning his "soul": "He said he had bent over it and that he had found nothing, gentlemen of the jury." The expression "gentlemen of the jury" legitimately belongs to a direct style; nevertheless it is placed in a sentence that reports words indirectly. This duality of styles in the same sentence indicates an ironic duality in the narrator; one might even ask if this duality can be termed duplicity in Meursault's case.

The simplest way of reckoning with this duality would be to see in it the duality between the author of the novel and the character of Meursault. In this second part of the narrative the author, we might say, has not succeeded in coinciding with his character as well as in the first portion. He wished to stress certain points, to give us a few winks, and by so doing has violated his character's point of view.

But, given the ground rule I adopted for this study, I have not allowed this kind of remark. I placed myself within a fiction according to which it is Meursault who has composed the book. Am I then to denounce in the duality just noted a duplicity on the part of Meursault, or can I account for this duality in a different manner? The examination of another difficulty will permit me to solve this one.

I am accepting the fiction that Meursault wrote the book. But then the question is raised: when did he write it? The narrative starts with "My mother died today." Thus I have the impression of dealing with a diary (an impression likely to be wrong, considering Meursault's character). However, this impression disappears during the second part of the narrative, when I read: "After I went to prison, I understood after a few days that I would never like talking about this period of my life." The first portion of the narrative thus would be written from day to day and would fit a period of spontaneous happiness: Meursault is living from day to day, from week to week. The second portion would be written after the fact, and would be appropriate for describing the period when Meursault has been led to reflect and to raise himself above daily experience in order to take a comprehensive view of things.

In fact, this opposition cannot be upheld. For in the first portion one finds, for instance, the following notation: "I think, now, that that was a false impression." And then too the fiction is more acceptable if one thinks that Meursault wrote, or spoke, all his narration after the fact, in his last hours (in the event of his not being pardoned). But then, how account for notations such as the "today" with which the narrative commences? It should be assumed that Meursault attempts to adopt two perspectives: he attempts to place himself both at the moment when he writes or speaks and at the moment when what he is narrating occurred.

Technically, what permits him to glide easily and without a break from one point of view to the other is, above all, the use of the past compound. The "I" subject of the verb is Meursault now, the narrator: it is he who remembers and comments. By means of the auxiliary verb we glide to the participle, which itself is enclosed within the past. Had the preterite been used, the verb would carry with it the subject into the past. The "I" of "I have done" is present, or rather a conscious presence. The "I" of "I did" is situated in a set of past occurrences. (What is strange in the "I" of Meursault the narrator is that this conscious presence is simply the presence, at least most frequently, of a cognitive consciousness: if this "I" is not objectified like the subject of the preterite, neither is it "subjective" in the usual manner of the subject of the compound past.)

This duality, or ambiguity, in perspective does not appear as duplicity: it suggests rather a desire for justness. Meursault attempts to find a language which correctly indicates from one point of view what happened, what he felt and thought at a given moment, and from another point of view what he is thinking and feeling as he narrates. Sometimes there is identity, and sometimes there is divergence. Broadly speaking, there is identity throughout the first part of the narrative, divergence during the second. An evolution in Meursault underlies occurrences in the plot: this evolution is concluded in a leap, by a flying forth in the last scene. Then, Meursault as narrated catches up with Meursault as narrator; this too is the moment in which Meursault attains a global view of his life, the ecstatic moment when the split between past and present ceases.

The duality or ambiguity in the point of view allows us to explain and justify the waverings and dissonances which could have disturbed us in the second portion of the narrative. During the trial Meursault presents himself as astonished, uncomprehending. He knows he is a criminal, he attempts to grow accustomed to the conventions that this implies socially, but the comedy of the tribunal, the sentimental and mythic language, are beyond his comprehension. He is prepared to understand what seems "natural" to him, but the order of the theatre seems unintelligible. As a matter of fact, if the word "comprehend" is taken in a narrow sense, what is comprehensible is the logical conduct—in harmony with his nature—of a living individual. But the theatre is antiphysis, belief is blindness, hypocrisy is mask, their language is overinflated: in a word, logos is perverted. We are in the realm of illogic, and illogic is, in itself, incomprehensible. It is only when one has admitted once and for all the illogical nature of the theatre, of belief, of hypocrisy and of consecrated and consecrating language that one may, in their particular manifestations, discover the logic of the theatre, of belief, of hypocrisy, and understand a rationale within the nonlogic. For instance, Meursault eventually understands how he is guilty in the eyes of theatrical society. And it is for this reason that during his narration he can appear at once naïve and ironic, as not understanding (the whole, at the very moment) and as understanding extremely well (details as he narrates).

During his imprisonment and trial Meursault attempts to adapt to his concrete condition of prisoner and to his social condition of criminal. It is in this perspective that it is appropriate to interpret sentences such as the following:

"When I left, I was about to offer him my hand, but just then I remembered that I had killed a man. . . . I was going to answer that that was precisely because it referred to criminals. But then I thought that I was like them myself. This was an idea I could not grow used to. . . . I could not understand why they deprived me of something that could do nobody any harm. Later on, I understood that that was part of the punishment. But by then I was growing accustomed to not smoking, so that the punishment was no longer a punishment to me. . . . Naturally, in the situation they had placed me I could not speak to anyone in that tone. I did not have the right to show affection or good will."

As we have seen, though, the word "criminal" is equivocal. It designates not only a legal state, but also a mythic persona. And when it is a question of social condition, it often is difficult to trace the dividing line between the legal and the mythic, between the law of the city and the law of opinion. This is already evident from the previous quotation. Interhuman convention is involved, and it introduces us to the order of the theatre.

However, Meursault has not grasped yet what he is in the eyes of theatrical society, what his persona represents. He has not yet felt what is religious in the word "guilty." In order to be aware of his guilty mask, he must abandon his own viewpoint and see himself through the eyes of the others or, rather, of the Other. This is difficult for him, in view of his temperament. An intuition, if not full intellection, of what he represents to theatrical society seems to come to him when he notices the reaction in the audience:

"He said I had not wanted to see my mother, that I had smoked, had slept, and that I had drunk some *café au lait.* Then I felt something rising throughout the courtroom and, for the first time, I understood that I was guilty."

This does not mean that Meursault *feels* guilty. Previously aware that he was a criminal, now he feels that he is religiously guilty in the eyes of theatrical society. But he does not internalize this mask of guilt, he does not assume responsibility. What he may experience is solitude. He will eventually assume this solitude, and even assert his right to it. In the second part of the narrative Meursault, facing the theatre, declared guilty by theatrical society, undergoes the experience of solitude. His evolution, from this point of view, is an internal progress into solitude.

Before imprisonment, Meursault felt neither alone nor not alone. True, he was living alone; in the detachment of his knowing consciousness he was alone; but he did not feel lonely. He maintained easy relations in his natural and social milieu, he was steeped in his milieu.

Imprisoned, Meursault undergoes a certain solitude, he experiences isolation. He is isolated in his cell, he is isolated from Marie and from things that he once loved. But this experience is neither definitive nor absolute: Meursault attempts to adapt himself to his new milieu.

On stage at the tribunal, the rites unfold in such a manner that Meursault receives the impression of being an "intruder," a "supernumerary." Thus there is a kind of ambiguity in his situation: it is his trial, yet everything happens as though there were a desire to exclude him from it. This ambiguity corresponds to the mythical condition of the guilty, of the scapegoat.

This ambiguity is again found in particular experiences. The witnesses for the defense, those who represent Meursault's adaptation to his human environment, participate in the action; but the court gets rid of them as soon as possible. Among the spectators of the trial, two show their interest in Meursault from their manner of watching him. There is first the young journalist of whom Meursault remarks:

"In his face, slightly assymetrical, I saw only the two bright eyes, very light, which were examining me attentively, expressing nothing definable. And I had the odd impression of being looked at by myself."

Instead of making Meursault feel with someone, and thus in some measure with the others, this solitary look causes Meursault to feel his loneliness, to make it interior and reflective.

There is also a woman who watches him "with intensity." Meursault has already encountered this woman at the restaurant, at which time she had appeared "odd" to him. He calls her "the automaton." The interest which this woman seems to take in Meursault can contribute to revealing his persona to him. Meursault is there on stage, but his role is that of a robot. A certain mask is fabricated for him, he is present for the purpose of having a mask affixed to his face, the mask of the guilty, the monster. The way in which this woman has struck him helps him grasp how he appears in the eyes of theatrical society.

Solitude proper to the condition of the guilty consists at once of being held and being rejected. It is an isolation under the look of others. It is being exhibited as a sacred mask. Meursault's situation is that of an idol, though this idol is designed to arouse a sacred horror and not sacred admiration (the word *sacer*, or *hagios*, indicates what provokes one reaction or the other). Meursault is rejected by the actors, nevertheless he is maintained on stage in the beam of a spotlight. This is what the reaction of the public reveals to him.

Meursault undergoes solitude. He as yet is not assuming it. The solitude of the guilty is imposed upon him. It is the solitude of the hero that he is going to claim.

To the paternalistic priest who would like Meursault to call him "my father," Meursault answers that he is not his father, that he is "on the others' side."

After being exhibited at the trial, pinned and rejected by the look of the others, Meursault is openly rejected by the sentence of death. But the ambiguity of this procedure is newly manifested by the intervention of the priest, who attempts to recover Meursault as a sinner, as a fallen creature, and to save him.

Meursault resists this temptation. The priest is "on the others' side." Meursault does not assume solitude out of guilt: it is precisely because he is guilty and is condemned that the priest attempts to redeem him, to draw him out of his solitude. Meursault has experienced the practical consequences of his mythical metamorphosis, but he does not assume the mask of guilt. A fortiori, he is not going to act as a sinner and play the publican's comedy. He has been told that he is guilty. Very well, that is settled. The condemnation throws him into solitude and in proximity to death: allow him then to assume solitude and the nearness of death.

We are nearing the last three pages of the narrative, the surge of anger which seizes Meursault and the final appeasement. There, we feel a leap. Meursault does not deny what he has been and what he has thought, but all that is placed in a new perspective. The underground motion which one divines in the course of this second part of the novel here becomes a leap. There are three points to note.

Meursault's violent apostrophe to the priest contains two of these points. For the moment let us set aside the first sentences of the apostrophe and examine the remainder, which contains the first point I wish to note:

"I had been right, I was still right, I was always right. I had lived in one way, and I could have lived in another. I had done this, and had not done that. I had not done one thing, because I was doing another. And so? It was as though I had all along been waiting for this moment, and this little dawn when I would be justified. Nothing, nothing had any importance, and I knew why. He too knew the reason. From the end of my future, throughout all this absurd life that I had led, an obscure breath had come back up toward me through the course of years which had not yet come about, and this breath in its passage equalized everything that had been proposed to me in the years I was living and which had no more reality. What did the death of others matter to me, or a mother's love, what did his God matter, the lives that are chosen, destinies that are elected, since only one destiny was to elect me and with me the billions of the privileged who, like him, called themselves my brothers. Could he understand, could he understand this? Everybody was privileged. There was nothing but the privileged. The others, too, they would be condemned some day. And he, too, would be condemned. What did it matter if, accused of murder, he was executed for not having wept at his mother's funeral? Salamano's dog counted as much as his wife. The little mechanical woman was as guilty as the Parisienne that Masson had married, or as Marie who wanted me to marry her. What did it matter that Raymond was my buddy as well as Celeste, who was a better man? What did it matter if Marie today should offer her mouth to a new Meursault? Did he understand, then, this condemned man, that from the depths of my future . . ."

The most obvious theme is that "nothing matters." This formula, though, is not so absolute as it seems. What does it refer to?

It attacks a theatrical conception of life. It attacks the sentimental and religious values. It attacks a conception according to which life would "have a meaning" coming to it from the outside (from collective myth), and according to which individuals and their destinies could be given grades by applying a collective table of values. Meursault rejects the mirage of antiphysis, and falls back upon physis. The label of guilt changes nothing about the fact of dying. The condemnation to death imparted by men is nothing but a theatrical gesture, for it is nature that condemns the individual to death.

Meursault's attack goes still further: it affects not only the theatre, but also what might exist outside the theatre; it attacks not only the collective myth, but also the personal myth whether or not it is imitative of the collective myth. This is seen in the passage: "What did it matter . . . the lives that are chosen, destinies that are elected." The value one wishes to grant his life by the choice of a personal myth, of a personal destiny, is only verbal. Destinies are of equivalent value; a destiny chosen in particular has no particular value, does not have the value which one wishes to confer it. Each one has a destiny; yet that does not mean that each man possesses his destiny, it means instead that each man is possessed by a destiny which is what it is and which could have been otherwise without alteration of its value (except for pleasantness). Thus, even though someone is chosen by a certain destiny one may say that the same

destiny chooses everyone, insofar as there is an
equality of value, or of nonvalue, if not an identity
of particular facts. Meursault deromanticizes, de-
tragedizes, in a word demythicizes the term "destiny"
by rendering it equivalent to "chance" or "necessity,"
the choice between these two terms mattering not in
the slightest. And this is in line with Epicurean wisdom leaning upon the physics of Democritus.

Yet the formula "nothing matters" is not so absolute as it appears. For why does Meursault become
angry? If nothing matters, the fact of believing or of
not believing in some god, in some myth, the fact of
believing or not believing in the theatrical "human"
values, the act of throwing oneself into the excess of
antiphysis or of holding oneself within the measure
of physis, the fact of thinking or of not thinking, of
saying or of not saying that nothing matters, has no
importance whatsoever. "Eppur si muove," as Galileo
said. But affirming or denying that the earth revolves,
what importance has that? The earth, whether one
affirms so or not, will continue to revolve, or not to
revolve.

Now, it is obvious from the first that something
has importance for Meursault, if only the affirmation
that nothing has any importance. In what way does
this matter? It cannot be the utilitarian importance of
a scientific truth, such as that recalled by the formula
"the earth revolves." Meursault does not attempt to
establish a scientific truth, he neither poses nor con-
ceives of himself as a martyr to truth. He defends
justness, his justness, a comprehension and not a
knowledge, the accord between his philosophy (his

91

thinking, his language) and his experience of life, and not the accord between a formula and the results of scientific experimentation. If one still wishes to speak of "truth" (Meursault uses this term at the beginning of his apostrophe), one must specify that he is speaking of an existential "truth," a verity of experience and not of experimentation, a "subjective" verity. In order to avoid miscomprehension, I prefer in such a case to speak of *justness*, for I have already remarked the moral importance that Meursault attached to the just use of language.

If he speaks with violence, it is because he is defending *himself*, because he is defending not an objective truth which could easily do without him, but the justness of his knowing consciousness, the justness of his Epicurean wisdom. He himself uses the word "justified."

The use of this word shows how Meursault's morals are opposed to the hypocritical morality (that is to say, the immorality) of theatrical men and their "justice." Meursault "was right" in adopting the point of view that he has adopted. "From the end of the future," the destiny that was to elect him was bringing a justification of his point of view, and now that that destiny has been accomplished Meursault feels justified even though he has been labeled guilty. And this moment when Meursault feels justified is the time chosen by the priest to tell him that he must justify himself in the eyes of the Christian God by denying himself!

However, in order to account for Meursault's violence, one must go deeper. I proceed to the second point. It is not only the reaction of the intellectual Meursault that we witness here, it is a reaction of his entire being. After all, Meursault has thought already that he was right as opposed to his employer concerning ambition, against Marie about marriage, against the examining magistrate in regard to religion. He reacted on those occasions without violence. But here Meursault is defending not only his intellectual justness, he is defending his living integrity. The beginning of the apostrophe suggests this:

"He seemed to be so very certain of everything. However, none of his certitudes was worth a single hair on a woman's head. He was not even certain of being alive because he was living like a dead man. As for me, I seemed to be facing the world with empty hands. But I was certain of myself, certain of everything, surer than he, certain of my life and of that death that was about to come. Yes, I had nothing other than that, but at least I held this truth as much as it held me."

The reference to a "hair on a woman's head" recalls something which, in the present, held some importance for Meursault. To theatrical values, to the extraterrestrial value of Paradise, Meursault opposes Epicurean value, terrestrial, sensual, and aesthetic. And here already are two kinds of things which have importance for Meursault: on one side justness of thought and language, on the other concrete things, sensual and aesthetic.

These two types of good have already been noted during the course of this study. Now, Meursault discovers a third which envelops these two, which is like their foundation, which is not on the same plane: there is a leap. What Meursault discovers is not the value of life in general terms but of his own life in particular. Until then there was the consciousness of Meursault witnessing things happening to him, pleasures and trouble. He now reaches an awareness of his life which is at once enveloping and intimate. He unites himself to his life, and totalizes it.

He has been led to recollect himself, to turn inward upon himself and to coincide with himself during his encounters with the theatre. He no longer floats within an indifferent or favorable human environment, he now is rejected into solitude. Men have become the others. In opposition, Meursault internalizes himself, coincides with himself. Condemnation to death leads him to consider his life as a whole, as a perfection not in the aesthetic connotation of the term but in the Greek meaning of the word "perfect." Meursault was living (imperfect), now he *has* lived (perfect); he still is living, but what he thinks he has to live is the have-lived. The life which he used to have to live, the future which was in the hands of destiny, the life of which he was not in possession, which had no value except in moments of pleasure, now becomes his own life, becomes value in its totality. Details do not matter as such, troubles do not matter as such, the error on the beach does not count as such. They have no more importance, nothing has any importance. But the totality, which Meursault holds and presses as if in his hands, has importance. Meursault possesses that, he has his life, he *has* lived it.

94

If one adopts a philosophy of projection and of action, largely a modern point of view, value is by preference placed upon the future. My life has value insofar as the future is open, insofar as my life opens to the future, insofar as I can project. Value is the value of the goal that I propose for myself. Sartre writes, for instance, "Value is what is not yet."

Meursault's philosophy is a philosophy of contemplation and of possession: he adopts, broadly speaking, an ancient point of view. His philosophy is one of having ("That was all I had") rather than a philosophy of doing. What has value is the possessed good. So long as he was living in the imperfect, value was represented by pleasures sensual and aesthetic in the actual, and by intellectual justness. Now that he is living in the perfect, intellectual justness has, so to speak, accomplished itself; it makes itself one with the value that Meursault's life becomes in its totality.

Thus the violence of Meursault's reaction is explained in a satisfactory manner. What the priest attempts to do, in Meursault's eyes, is to steal from him that life which has become his good in the face of death, to take away the value which has revealed itself against the background of death. Caught within his belief, the priest does not conceive of this life except as a preparation for God's judgment. This life, in its totality, is thus conceived of as a labor, whereas, for Meursault, it has its end in itself and thus justifies itself, in the manner of a game. This opposition between life conceived globally as labor and life conceived globally as a game is inherent in the opposition which has been presented in the "Christian" schema and in the "pagan." The priest tries to give life a value that transcends it. But in so doing he alienates his life: it will never be his own. Labor can have validity to the extent that it permits play. Labor is justified by play. But the justification and the compensation for which the priest searches are not within his hands: they are in the hands of a God supposed to dispose of them as it pleases Him. It is thus by wishing to grant life a value which transcends it that the priest, in the eyes of Meursault, whisks away the value that could be had by living in either the imperfect or the perfect. For life, in the priest's perspective, is never something which it is possible to enjoy. To the priest who asks him how he would imagine another satisfying life, Meursault responds: "A life where I could remember this one," in which, that is, he could enjoy this earthly and past life as an acquired good. In wishing to deny death, in positing an immortality, the priest is led to deaden the moments of this life, as Meursault relates. The latter values his death as much as his life. For his life cannot be totalized except against the background of death. Laying claim to his living integrity, Meursault is led to lay a claim upon his death. To be fully alive is to be fully mortal.

Before passing to the third point, two remarks concerning apparent incoherences in the text should be made.

At the conclusion of his apostrophe, Meursault presents the theme of universal condemnation to death. Everyone is condemned to death by the fact of living. However, a moment before, the priest had sketched the same theme in order to draw Meursault closer, and Meursault retorted, "That's not the same thing." There is a difference between Meursault's destiny and that of the priest, because the former seems accomplished whereas the latter does not seem yet so. Meursault is living in the perfect while the priest is on "the others' side," living in the imperfect. Meursault is living the have-lived whereas the others are living the have-to-live. At the end of his apostrophe, on the contrary, Meursault considers mortals, including now himself, in the frame of having-to-live-and-die. And he can adopt this point of view because destiny has been accomplished for himself.

Second, it is fitting to reconcile the two parts that I distinguished in the apostrophe. In the second part, Meursault gives an identity of nonvalue to the various destinies. He even speaks of "this absurd life" which he says he has lived. In the first portion, his life is presented as a value. In the second portion, Meursault adopts the priest's point of view, which attempts to give life a value from the exterior. Life then would receive a value from something other than itself, in the way work receives value from some end which surpasses it: I do not work for the sake of working but, for example, in order to make money. But what could life be, considered from the outside? It might be the concept of life in general: an essence, or else what concerns the biologist. In comparing lives and destinies, one tends to establish a scale of values. But in the name of what? Even though we are concerned with particular lives, even yet we are dealing in abstractions since we wish to give this or that life a value in a comparative manner, that is to say, still from the outside. Considered thus, Meursault's life, *like* those of other people, is, in his words, absurd; that is, without value. But considering life—even one life—from the exterior is not living it. From the point of view of the biologist or of some god, a life is not a lived life. In order to consider one life as a lived life, I must either be the one living it or I must imaginatively place myself in the stead of whoever is living it as he lives it (which, obviously, is only partially possible). It is this intimate point of view that Meursault adopts at the beginning of his apostrophe. His life, doubtless, is absurd but that does not mean that it is lacking "value." I would say that the life that I am living has no *meaning,* for it is *sense,* sense being the foundation or reference of all meanings. My life as I live it has no meaning in reference to anything else; things have, or lack, meaning and value in reference to myself. For Meursault, his life itself, as he *has* lived it, has value, or rather, is the value. Let us return to the opposition of work and play. For someone who does not know how to play chess, a game of chess is absurd; it amounts to pushing pieces of carved wood over a board with black and white squares. But the game has value as it is played, and the total game of life is the value.

There remains a third point to develop. After his violent reaction to the demand that he deny himself, Meursault attains a final appeasement, his *analysis:*

"There, over there too, around that home where lives were being snuffed out, the evening was like a melancholy truce. So near to death, Mother must have

98

felt liberated and ready to live everything over again. Nobody, nobody had any right to weep over her. And I too, I felt ready to live everything over again. As if this great anger had purged me of evil, emptied of hope, before this night filled with signs and stars, I opened myself up for the first time to the tender indifference of the world. Finding it so like myself, at last so brotherly, I felt that I had been happy, and that I was still happy. For everything to be consummated, to feel less alone, I was left with hoping that there would be many spectators the day of my execution, and that they would greet me with cries of hate."

"Liberation" must not be interpreted in the frame of a philosophy of doing, for then it would mean disengagement from hindrances and the possibility of being engaged in a certain means of realization. "Liberation" would mean the opening of the future, the real possibility of a choice previously denied. But, in the framework of Meursault's philosophy, "liberation" means the end of the control of destiny upon Meursault (and over his mother). Meursault is no longer possessed by the destiny of things to come, for destiny in his eyes has accomplished itself. Now, Meursault feels that he possesses his life. There is a reconciliation, or better a coincidence, between Meursault and his destiny, which has become his life. Thus he can say that he would be ready "to live everything over again," that is to live in the perfect a life that he has lived from day to day. He would be ready to relive as a whole a life that he has been able to live only in detail. "Relive" does not mean to live a life as it was lived, for that would not be reliving. The repetition marked by the prefix of the verb "relive" shows a passage from the plane of the imperfect to that of the perfect, from details to a constituted whole. By reliving his life, Meursault would live it in possession of his destiny, something of which he was incapable while he was living it. This would be living as one remembers, or as one feels on the occurrence of *déjà vu*. Meursault's narration gives us an idea of such reliving. Within this frame, the compound past of the narrative ought to be interpreted as a perfect.

This difference between to live and to relive, between living what there is to live and living what has been lived, accounts for the apparent incoherence between the end of the first portion of the narrative and the conclusion of the second. At the time of its occurrence, the act upon the beach had appeared to Meursault as an error that brought about misfortune. Later on, this error and this leap into misfortune have developed into the test of imprisonment, of the theatre, and of the nearness of death. Now that he has triumphed over his ordeals, dissonance fades. Error has become accomplished fact, a neutral occurrence under the same rubric as other events. Error and misfortune have become part of destiny and, as Meursault assumes this destiny which previously was in possession of him, a liberation is produced, a reconciliation. On the strength of his recaptured ataraxia, Meursault can pronounce his beautiful pagan epitaph: "I felt that I had been happy, and that I was still happy."

Meursault has attained the two principal objectives fixed by Epicureanism: he has overcome the fear of death and he has divested himself of the fear of the gods (or, more precisely, he has refused to believe in a judicial God). The words I have just quoted recall Epicurus' letter of farewell: "I am writing this letter on a happy day of my life which is also my last day."

Meursault now manages to live according to nature on a new plane. Until now, he had been attempting to think and speak according to nature, according to justness, and he had attempted to enjoy whatever the moment concretely presented to him. Now the two are joined on a new plane. His destiny being accomplished such as he sees it, his life totalized, he realizes a global coincidence with his nature. Facing death, Meursault's accord with his own nature (by the assumption of this totalized life) is also an accord with nature itself. Meursault experiences an accord between his totalized life and the night sky that he contemplates. He opens himself up to "the tender indifference of the world." Meursault's ataraxia is in accord with the ataraxia of physis. He is devoid of hope and hope appears to him as evil, in that it prevents life from totalizing as an enveloping physis. To hope is to become the prey of what is to come. By "indifference" Meursault understands "liberation from hope," and not "insensibility." Meursault loves life, exalts life even, but so far as it is his own.

Nocturnal physis is felt as being "like" Meursault's life, as "brotherly," and not as maternal or paternal. Meursault does not adopt an attitude of respect or of adoration before physis. Physis is not designed to provide a meaning, or a value, to Meursault's life, as would a creative, legislative, and judicial God. There is harmony, there is equivalence and similarity.

Here physis is the starry night. Meursault notes not only "stars" but "signs" as well. But these signs do not indicate an architect, or the watchmaker of cosmologic proofs, they do not ordain destinies, they do not limit the distances in a mathematical universe. At most, for Meursault these signs seem to resemble him. Meursault's life is totalized like a sky of stars. This life and this sky are not aesthetically perfect. It does not in the least matter that this star or that fact is here and not elsewhere, exists or does not exist. There is neither the idea of order nor the idea of disorder. There is a satisfaction in contemplating the heavens and in the possession of life because both appear achieved, necessary because accomplished, stable, freed from becoming. The sky is absurd, as is Meursault's life. But like Meursault's life, it does not have to receive meaning from anything. It is a sovereign and serene apparition, it is a totality that is.

Thus Meursault finally reaches the "shade and the fountain" for which, overwhelmed by heat and blinded by sunlight, he had searched that noon at the beach. The starry night is this shade and this spring. It is, so to speak, a dry spring to which Meursault opens himself. It purifies him, accomplishes him in his stature and in his justness. "The arid psyche," said Heraclitus, "is the highest and the most just."

102

Yet Meursault still must appear before men. "For everything to be consummated," he must take part in the ceremony of public execution. He has chosen the part of nature against the theatre. He has passed beyond the solitude into which he was thrust. Now he feels that physis is brotherly, but of course physis is not another person as a brother would be. Meursault simply, as in the past, feels neither alone nor not alone. Thus when he hopes for a large attendance to his execution, "so that I shall feel less alone," one is tempted to conclude that he is ironic because what Meursault is asking of the spectators is a manifestation of hate, not of compassion. "Nobody had the right to weep about her," he said of his mother; the last sentence indirectly says the same thing of his own case.

The intention of the last sentence may not be wholly ironic. Meursault mentions the others, he has not forgotten other people. He takes a position of defiance in regard to the human theatre. He is not content to leave in the hands of others the mask of the guilty and of the monster that they have fashioned for him. He does not lose sight of himself in the eyes of men, he maintains himself in the human perspective for himself and for the sake of others, those, for example, who might read his narrative.

I now must, to conclude, attempt to justify the title of this chapter: "the hero." The word "hero" has various applications. It designates at the beginning a demigod in Greek mythology. Now it often designates the principal character of a novel. By "hero" I shall

103

mean someone who assumes an exemplary destiny. This implies someone who assumes that destiny is an exemplary manner.

I must specify what I mean by "exemplary." How is the destiny of a hero exemplary? One speaks of exemplary destinies, or of exemplary lives, in reference to men who, it is thought, have devoted, indeed "sacrificed" their lives to some "cause": to science, to a nation, to religion or, as it is said, to "humanity." In such cases exemplarity is allegorical: the individual incarnates a certain abstraction, a certain myth. The man in question, from the viewpoint of the imitative theatrical morality, is a model. The man whom I call a hero must be distinguished from the man who is made to appear, rightly or wrongly, as a comedian or tragedian taking his role, his persona, too seriously. When I speak of an exemplary destiny, I do not mean an exemplary role. Assuming a destiny is not the same as playing a role in the repertory.

I could say that the destiny of the hero is exemplary and that the hero assumes it in an exemplary manner insofar as this destiny and its assumption by the hero eminently reveal something fundamental and specific in the human condition. The human condition must not be conceived of as a form, as an essence, as a role to play, as a cause to uphold. Among other things, the expression "the human condition" implies uniqueness. The human condition is not a theatrical essence which would ideally exist before the hero and which that hero would incarnate. I have stated that the hero's destiny and its assumption eminently reveal the human condition. One must make it clear that this revelation is an invention. The hero, as I see him, is not necessarily "heroic" in the commonplace acceptance of that term. Being human is being condemned to assume uniqueness. Through stupidity, hypocrisy, because of social and material strangleholds, most of us, I presume, spend our time ignoring, or masking, or denying our uniqueness. The hero lays claim to it, and brings it into the full light of day.

To be sure, my use of the word "exemplary" implies that there is something to be learned. But if the hero is exemplary from this viewpoint, he is not so as a model for imitation. In the same way, saying of a poet that he is exemplary does not mean that to learn from him is to parody him. Unlike a martyr, the hero does not consecrate one dogma or another, this or that cause, this or that standard virtue. He is exemplary in that he encourages me to assume my own identity, to invent the human condition on my own account. The hero does not hypnotize; whether I feel myself near or far in relation to him, he encourages me to liberate myself, to accomplish myself.

Here is how the connection between this conception of the hero and the original conception may be presented. The mythical hero is a demigod. He adds something to the Pantheon, to what already was clearly, stably, and permanently existing. Whereas animal life is the simple prey of destiny, the hero erects something above this plane, on a "divine" plane, but according to his nature as a man, by assuming his destiny.

I have presented Meursault within the framework of paganism and of Epicureanism. But this is an intellectual schema, a classification which works from the outside. Meursault's intention was not at all to consecrate Epicureanism, to be the Epicurean martyr, or to incarnate the essence of Epicureanism. And if the manner in which Meursault assumes his destiny offers a lesson, this lesson does not consist in an inducement to believe in the "truth" of Epicureanism at the exclusion of all other intellectual schemas. What Meursault accomplishes is his own authenticity, and it happens that his manner of realizing authenticity appears to me from the outside as a pagan type, more precisely, Epicurean. The unique is unique from within. Seen from the outside, it appears as individual, hence classifiable and subject to labeling by generalities.

In recapitulating the results of my study, it remains to show briefly how Meursault's destiny appears exemplary, and the exemplary manner in which Meursault assumes his destiny.

In order that a destiny appear destiny, and an exemplary destiny, it must form a certain striking figure and this figure must reveal something fundamental. Expressions like "tragic irony" and "poetic justice" allude to such figures. I have indicated, concerning this, the harmonious opposition between Meursault and his judges, between his nature and the theatre, between the first and second portions of the narrative. A metaphysical innocent is declared theatrically guilty, by virtue of this innocence. An individual who esteems justness of thought and language is condemned for exactly that by human "justice"; and the condemnation is to death. The revealed absurdity forms a figure. The particular absurdity of Meursault's destiny is exemplary.

Let us proceed to the second point. Meursault does not assume his destiny by attempting to direct it, to prophesy it, to force it. He is not what I would call a romantic hero. I mean by that someone who decides to live his life and who lives it as if it were a work of art to be created. "Nature" is then conceived of as a kind of inspiration. Subjective infiniteness attempts to actualize itself. Destiny is forced. But it must be forced in such a manner that objectivity reveals its insufficiency in relation to subjectivity. It is, if it may be said, the essential dissatisfaction which must be satisfied. The revelation of this insufficiency may be viewed in several ways. The goal, once attained, once become result, will be presented derisively; it is the occasion of a properly romantic irony. Or again the hero will envision a goal impossible to attain, and he will adopt it precisely because it is impossible to attain. Or then again the revelation of subjectivity will be envisioned in a certain kind of death, that is in the abolition of subjectivity simultaneously with objectivity. This is the case of the legendary criminal who vowed to die upon the scaffold. It is also the case of Jesus, according to a possible interpretation of the Evangelists. Or again the aim will be madness, beyond the wall of the impossible. It probably was what tempted Rimbaud.

Nothing like this with Meursault. He does not force his destiny, he does not conceive of his life as a work to realize, he does not choose his death. In his manner of seeing things, life-to-live is absurd, destiny selects

107

the living, a living man does not select his destiny. One can of course say that by this conception Meursault appropriates his destiny in advance, whatever it might be. But that would be only an empty intellectual appropriation. It shows us Meursault as a sage and not as a hero.

It is only during his last moments, in the leap that I have noted, that Meursault may be called a hero, that he assumes his destiny in an exemplary manner. It is no longer a question of a simple adaptation to circumstances, of a resignation to death. Meursault exalts life, not life in general but his own. He makes it his own and exalts it even when from the outside he declares it absurd. And he makes it his own and exalts it against the background of death. Meursault affirms himself, establishes himself, in the silence and the plenitude of a starry night.

This is the divine aspect. But even at this moment he affirms and establishes himself as a man, and he is conscious that his establishment is not of a thing but of a living being, of a human individual. His last sentence, not to mention the fact of his narration, shows that he is establishing himself in relation to men, and in relation to the human condition. The hero is alone, but his solitude is exemplary. He integrates himself, accomplishes himself and grows silent, but his tacit integrity provides a halo for language. He closes about his life, comprehends himself in the act, yet by so doing, he opens to us the possibility of a comprehension in language.

NOTE TO THE
AMERICAN EDITION

Reading the English translation makes me return to this essay twelve years after writing it. I had designed it to react against a conception of Meursault which was still current at the time: someone with no values, a likely personification of the ideas on the absurd formulated in *The Myth of Sisyphus;* an exemplification of a mythical Modern Man and of a new *mal du siècle.* So I soaked my Meursault in the venerable essences of Greek tradition and classical values.

A piece of fiction is like a set of axioms: the commentator tries to draw theorems out of them, testing their coherence and fecundity in the process. This way of speaking should, of course, be taken with a grain of salt: words are not mathematical symbols. With this reservation in mind, I still think that, on the whole, my essay is faithful to *The Stranger.*

Meursault had to be pried away from *Sisyphus.*

The styles of life which are sketched in Camus' first essay hardly agree in atmosphere and internal economy with Meursault's own style. True, *The Myth of Sisyphus* alludes, at one point, to a "postal supernumerary." This might be an opening for a Meursault type. But the example is not developed. Given the tone of the essay, it could not.

In *The Myth of Sisyphus* and in *Man in Revolt*, Camus gives free rein to his oratorical talent. Yet he mistrusted this talent and became somewhat ashamed of its spell. In *The Stranger*, he reacts against it; also in *The Plague*, with much less success in my opinion: to my taste, *The Plague* is academically dull. In *The Fall*, a dramatic monologue in the line of Louis-René des Forêts' *Bavard*, he adopts another tactic: full-blown oratory again, but the responsibility is shifted from author to character. Convenient, perhaps too convenient. But, if self-criticism is recognized in *The Fall*, it should be seen that the basic criticism bears ironically on the chosen style.

Reacting against a certain conception of Meursault, I had to adopt the approach of what I reacted against. This was a rule of the game. Extracting dispositions from narrated process, I had to neglect the differences between fiction and history. Judging from certain traces in my essay, it bothered me a bit. It would bother me more now. I have been working on a philosophy of literature which tries to link modes of meaning with modes of existence. This has made me more and more sensitive to the divergences between historical and fictional existence.

The Stranger derives some of its original impact

110

from its being narrated in the first person. But what happens on a second, third, fourth reading, as the aesthetic perspective tends to purify and stabilize itself? I wonder now whether the third person would not have been preferable.

I am not suggesting a return to what is badly called the omniscient author, badly called because, strictly speaking, fictional events are not a matter of knowledge: unlike a historical report or prediction, the basic narration in a novel can be neither true nor false; it is axiomatic. And I am not suggesting that it would have been better to have a character other than Meursault carry the point of view. Observer is one thing, narrator another, narration still another.

All three are needed in a historical perspective. Only observer and narration are necessary in fiction. Much of the contemporary theorizing about narrative fiction appears based on a flaw: the confusion between narrator and narration, the postulate that, if there is a narration, there must be a narrator, instead of just a fictional observer to carry the point of view. Hence the trouble when no narrator is posited as a speaking or writing character situated in the fictional space-time. If you, the commentator, insist on adding a narrator, will he be fictional or historical? You will be obliged to do as if he were both and neither. You will, in other words, create a mythical character. This way of proceeding goes with an unawareness of the differences between historical and fictional conditions. It may also be seen as a relic from the days of the epic, when history and fiction remained indistinguished in legend, when the story was actually told

111

by someone before your eyes, whose voice you could hear: compare, in recent criticism, the use of "voice," instead of "narrator," where "tone" would be enough. The novelists themselves have contributed to the situation, reluctant as they were, and still are, to leave history to history.

To return to *The Stranger.* How could a third person narrative, that is to say a narration using Meursault as the only point of view, but not as a narrator, have been preferable?

First, it should have made Camus more wary of certain ways of saying things which do not seem to fit in with a Meursault system, at least as I view this system (Camus was kind enough to approve of my interpretation, but this is largely irrelevant). I am not alluding to the beach episode, which does not bother me in this respect, but to certain stylistic touches here and there, which strike me as false notes.

Second, we would not have to wonder when and where Meursault tells his story. No doubt, we do not have to assume that he writes it or that he tells it to someone other than himself. But changes in tenses, added to the use of the first person, oblige us to posit him as a narrator, which makes the question of time and place legitimate. I broached the question in my essay. Other commentators have pursued it. None of the solutions strikes me as satisfactory and I don't think there can be a satisfactory solution. The reason is this: whatever the solution, the moment and place, or moments and places, of Meursault's storytelling must be determined. And they are not determined by the narration. Which shows that the set of axioms is not closed. The use of the third person would close it.

Third, granted again my Meursault system, it does not seem quite fitting that Meursault should bother to tell his own story, even to himself. And the system cannot be modified so as better to accommodate this storytelling feature of Meursault. For this would require a decision as to the time and place of the telling.

The Stranger has ontological and ethical significance. Which is as it should be. The relation of literature, and philosophy, to cognitive and practical language, as we use it and as it uses us day after day, is critical in a Kantian sense. The significance of literature is not in opposition to, but defined by, its aesthetic nature. It varies according to the mode of meaning. The critical angle of narrative fiction differs from the critical angles of drama and of analysis.

Narrative fiction bears critically on narrative nonfiction: the various forms of reporting, history, biography, autobiography. Its ontological reach is measured by the importance of time and space, its ethical reach by the tie between cognitive and practical: reported facts are facts as reported (selection, inferences, decoupage, montage, wardrobe, make-up); facts are reported to persuade and influence.

The ontological and ethical significance we grant to a given work depends on our interpretation and on our ontology and ethics. What modes of existence do you recognize? What do you hold to be deep, fundamental? What do you consider as ethically good, bad, indifferent?

Ethical significance involves another type of question, scientific rather than philosophical: what influence can a given work have on the readers' behavior? We make guesses based on hearsay and on our own experience. We assume that the influence of a certain work may be ethically decisive. But, at present, our scientific knowledge on this subject is nil. Many factors would seem to come into play, which lend themselves badly or not at all to experimental juggling: temperament, intelligence, culture; temporary psychophysiological states; economic, social, and political conditions; other books read (other conditions being equal, a book X might have effect A if read after book Y and effect B if read before; and the same book might have a different effect on second reading).

I read *The Stranger* for the first time in London toward the end of the Second World War. I should say that, if it had any effect then, it acted on me as a tonic. In 1958, at a colloquium which I attended, a British philosopher reported the case of a student who had become frightfully depressed after reading *The Stranger.* And I have a vague recollection of two newspaper articles which stated that *The Stranger* was among the books read by two persons not long before they committed suicide. In each case, are we entitled to posit a cause and effect relation? Our information is too scanty. Besides, even if we assume such a relation to hold, this still leaves the ethical question undecided. We have to decide whether the tonic effect was ethically good, bad, or indifferent. The same goes for the kind of depression claimed in the second example; and note that, in this particular case, the

114

philosopher said that he made a successful application of philosophical therapeutics by pointing out what his protégé had failed to see in *The Stranger*. Even if, *per impossibile*, all relevant factors were known, we should still have to decide, in the third example, whether suicide is ethically indifferent, or always good, or always bad, or sometimes good, sometimes bad.

As late as 1961, a critic expressed the opinion that Meursault is "a stranger to all normal human emotions and experiences." Try "normal" in a statistical sense. Meursault manifests a taste for restraint in speech. This does appear abnormal. But what of his heterosexual leanings? Statistically, they should be normal. Which makes me wonder: is the ethical theory, or practice, of the critic such that he considers sexual emotion and experience ethically abnormal, that is to say, bad, insofar at least as they have something to do with the opposite sex?

Ethical significance is part of the aesthetic worth of a novel. Looking for structure is useful; but, with a little ingenuity, some kind of structure can be found in anything. The artistic coherence of a piece of fiction involves semantics as well as grammar. In order to be consonant, it has to be resonant. Ethically, it has to appeal to values which resonate in the reader's sensibility. It may help the reader to bring out the latent. It may help him see more clearly certain sociolinguistic habits as ethically bad or indifferent. It may show, through aesthetic contrast, conflicts between values. It may suggest a reshuffling, fusions and disjunctions, displacements in application.

The writer may do all this more or less neatly and cogently, according to his medium: a fictional hero should not look like a walking treatise of ethics. The reader may react strongly or weakly, honestly or dishonestly, for or against. He may implicitly consider the piece of fiction as a satisfactory realization of the values involved. The phrases "aesthetic contrast" in the preceding paragraph, and "ethical colors" in the next, show the threat of aestheticism: think of the nice part given to the concept of evil in metaphysical tradition. Literature is then used as an alibi.

Playing the reaction game, my essay here and there hammers at the obvious, or overstresses the not so obvious. A few readers took it for a comprehensive formulation of my own ethics. Not so. But composing a portrait of Meursault in ethical colors appeared a worthwhile exercise at the time.

Robert J. Champigny

January, 1969